Echoes of Understanding

Soul-Reflecting Words for Your Unspoken Heart

SPROUT
PUBLISHING

Copyright © 2023 Teesha Michaels

ISBN: 9798857052532

All rights reserved.

No part of this publication may be reproduced, distributed, or transmitted in any form or by any means, including photocopying, recording, or other electronic or mechanical methods, without the prior written permission of the publisher, except in the case of brief quotations embodied in critical reviews and certain other noncommercial uses permitted by copyright law.

FROM THE HEART

Within this sacred tribute, my heart's ink flows onto the pages, crafting an ode to my extraordinary mother. She stands as an unwavering pillar, supporting my very existence and radiating goodness, forever illuminating the path before me.

Through her, I received an abundance of priceless teachings, akin to carefully bestowed gems, casting their wisdom upon my journey. Guided by her light, I ventured towards the hidden purpose nestled deep within my being. With each revelation, she untangled the intricate web of life, unraveling its mysterious threads and unveiling the grand design awaiting my discovery. This concealed purpose, a sacred calling to my soul, encompasses a profound connection to others, a transformative odyssey of self-realization, and the pursuit of a meaningful contribution to the world around me.

My mother, an alchemist of life, emerged triumphant from the depths of adversity. Unfazed by her humble origins, she defied the boundaries imposed by circumstance and transformed her existence from barren soil to an enchanting garden. Her resilience and unwavering spirit echo the legacy she inherited from her own mother, my beloved grandma. An angelic presence, suffused with boundless love, my grandmother's warmth permeated every fiber of her being.

To my precious daughters, may this timeless message reach your souls, awakening the infinite worth that resides within. You are treasures beyond measure, forever cherished in my heart. Yet, more importantly, I yearn for you to believe in your own limitless potential, regardless of life's tribulations. You possess the power to shape and nurture your own happiness, to uncover the enchantment that life bestows upon you. I witness the marvel twinkling in your eyes, as vibrant as the morning sun, for you are merely tiny tots. May that sense of wonder, that magical perspective, forever blaze brightly, even in the face of adversity. May these words resound in your lives someday, rekindling that childlike wonder when you need it most. Your existence has epitomized the very essence of beauty in this world, and for that, my gratitude knows no bounds, eternally grateful for your presence.

And to my soul sisters, my dearest confidantes, your stories and resilience continue to astound me. You are warriors, forged from flames and sprinkled with pixie dust. Despite the shadows that have embraced you, you steadfastly emerge as luminous beacons in this world. This book, a mosaic of shared experiences, is dedicated to all of you and to every soul in need of solace. Within these heartfelt echoes, etched from the deepest recesses of my being, lie words meant for everyone to embrace and find comfort in.

CONTENTS

Introduction 8

The Journey of Self 15

Breaking the Chains of Self Division 18

Welcoming Harmony: Trusting the Flow of Life's Journey ... 23

Love's Unveiling: Seeking Belonging and Happiness Within 35

Beyond Measure: Discovering Intrinsic Worth and Authentic Value 41

The Paradox of Self-Definition and Connection 50

Release and Renewal: (re)Building Yourself 64

Reinvention, Growth, and the Ever-Unfolding Self 76

Discovering Inner Anchors 84

Choosing Joy: From the Pinnacle to the River's Edge 97

Beyond Achievement: The Joy of Being 103

The Art of Stillness: Finding Serenity in the Present 110

Discovering Your Intrinsic Purpose 120

Embodied Love: Beyond Theory, Into Being 132

Unveiling the Essence of Existence 138

The Inner Sanctuary: Embracing Self-Love 148

Reclaiming the Source Within 158

Love as the Guiding Compass: Following the Way Home 167

21 Echoes of Understanding: *Golden Principles for Self-Love and Acceptance* 175

Conclusion..182

Epilogue 188

INTRODUCTION

Once upon a time, the universe told a story...

It was a spontaneous act of creativity, simply because it is the nature of our universe to be creative and to be spontaneous.

The tale arrived one day, seed-like, perfect, full of magic, and to the amazement and delight of everyone present. The plot of this story took a long time to develop; it's still not ultimately finished, and perhaps it never will be.

It is a wonderful story. It's one of those classic sagas that are full of plot twists and human emotions, it has all these ups and downs, and there is a lovable character at the heart of it all.

There are dark moments in the tale; there are also uplifting moments, crazy incidents, and lots of surprises. Even though some of the story feels uneventful, even in the dullest parts, in those chapters stretching between those big life-changing events, there are moments of such wonder sprinkled between the lines that it takes your breath away. Every page is worth the read. Each distinct frame of the movie reel is a work of art. It is exquisitely complicated.

It's a story of the most miraculous detail, and best of all is the character development of the protagonist. The main character in the story learns so much and gets to discover a big secret in the end.

There are unlikely friendships, strange coincidences, and unexplained kindnesses, along with heartwarming days, failures, betrayals, lies, forgiveness, successes—and so much more besides. There's a deep spiritual subtext. There's romance, comedy, action, and lots of fantasy. There's something uniquely human and something quite unexplainable about this story.

It's one of a kind.

Do you know this story?

It's the story of you.

The universe is writing it at this very moment… and somehow, weirdly enough, it's also the story of me! You see, we're all connected in this series of events, like stars arranged into massive galaxies. We all flow and swirl together. To tell the story of you fully, we have to include the stories of millions upon millions of beings, otherwise, none of our stories would make sense.

If this story had a beginning at all, then the beginning is lost somewhere very far back in the flow of time. As with all the best stories, the end is already implicit in the beginning—and so it is with our story too.

In case you are wondering what this story is all about: It's about your whole life and it explains your particular place in the great tapestry of stories that makes up one giant LIFE, the one great tale of forever.

Just imagine it. What if everything that we are is a story that the universe is telling itself. Every human life is a brand-new twist in the plot. Who gets to decide what kind of a story my life is going to be?

This tale is all about that curious thing that we are referring to when we say "I." It's a reflection of a reflection. It is an echo of understanding. We get to understand what it is truly like to live—as "I."

Have you ever stopped to think about what that little word actually means? I think it takes a lifetime to know the deepest meaning. Maybe it takes many lifetimes. Maybe if we collected everyone's story, and put them into a great big book, they would overlap and show us what it means to be conscious and what it means to love, despite incredible odds.

If this is the story of "me," then it must also be the story of the true self, and it means that this strange cosmic love story includes everyone that has ever lived and everything that has ever happened. It has to be so because each separate thing implies every other thing.

Could my story exist without yours? Could your story exist without mine? All things are intertwined, and the plots of our stories meet and intersect. They knit together with one another. We are characters in the stories of everyone we know and they are characters in our story too. Together we weave our threads together into a beautiful patchwork, the Grand Master story of what it means to be human.

For billions of years this cosmic folk tale has been going on and the project is far from finished.

We are living art, we are dreaming, thinking, breathing mysteries, we are walking paradoxes—and after all this time, there's still a lot to discover. Our narratives are still being written. New themes are being explored. Old plot ideas are being reinvented. Classic stories never go out of fashion, but even those keep on changing, in subtle ways, one lifetime after another, after another...

Just imagine! Billions of years ago, the atoms that now clothe our human forms were forged in a fiery star, somewhere in the depths of the vast, light-dappled canvas of space-time.

We are these mesmerizing arrangements of stardust and hope, strung together on a frame of bones, with graceful necks connected to fragile heads that are filled with crazy ideas. Without that fiery stellar beginning, we could not have been what we are today.

We are moving receptacles of wonder for the mysteries streaming from the great beyond of space, rooted to the earth by the miracle soles of our feet, transmitting that feeling of awe back to Mamma Earth. She loves the way our feet tickle her skin...

Even today, those mysterious points of energy, our atoms, our molecules—they still change and adapt, they move and they dance—with us. They love to be us. They are ancient, those tiny atoms, and they have danced the dance of the centuries with us. The unexplainable force that binds our atoms into our human shapes is even older, and I am willing to bet that there are a few big surprises for us in the distant future...

For millions of years now, our human DNA has changed and adapted. The experiences that forged our inner physical blueprint included great storms, ice ages, earthquakes, wars, many lifetimes, and a thousand other challenges. The world-mind that we share was forged by countless stories, countless hardships, shared by millions upon millions of weird people. All those challenges...

You overcame them all.

The journey that has brought each of us to where we are now is an incredible tale! So many details had to be just right in order for us to exist as we do. So many complicated plot twists had to turn out just as they did, so that we could be born, so that we could be alive, here and now.

Through fire and ice, evolution and revolution, one challenge after another, our cells stored the wisdom and passed it to our collective children, who passed them to their own children. Our great-great-great-grandparents passed on those lessons and our parents passed that ancient living wisdom on to us.

Every failure informed the collective. Every tragedy showed us a truth—how not to live our lives. Even in our ugliest, most heartless moments, humanity showed a kind of cosmic beauty. We had the strength to heal, and learn, and transcend...

The pathway that led to this—the beings we are today—included the path of the warrior, the path of the mother, the path of the healer, the farmer, the hunter, the gatherer, the fool, the hero, and the villain. It was the path of the survivor, the path of the artist, and the path of every human being in our own personal lineages. We carry that sacred, very human blueprint, and one day we might pass it on again.

At this point in our journey through the millennia, we happen to look like sentient human beings and it's still a work in process. Each day we change. Every day each of us is becoming what we need to be to fit the moment. Every single day we start a new page in the story of "me."

CHAPTER 1

THE JOURNEY OF SELF

I am flow,

I am returning to my source, a rippling stream of life,

I am a dancing wisp of energy pouring into the ocean of life.

I am forever becoming, and forever disappearing,

Moment by moment, here and now,

How strange it seems that every morning I wake

and recognize the face in the mirror.

"Hello me!" I might say to that face.

Am I still here?

What will I become today?

Then, if I look deeply into those eyes looking straight back at me in the mirror, I might wonder. "What is this deep mystery, what is the essence of this living conundrum that stares back at itself? Who am I, really? What am I worth? What will I become?"

Perhaps I will never know. Maybe the whole point of me is to ask the question, and to find a new answer, just for today.

For I am alive. I am life itself, experiencing life as me. I am a conscious being, looking at the being of the universe. I am intelligent awareness, aware of the whole cosmos, which I can sense, is aware of me.

Seen from this universal perspective, my usual idea of "me" seems a bit lightweight.

What are my self-criticisms about my weight, my height, my hair color and the shape of my nose, when considered from this cosmic perspective? Don't they seem a bit out of place? Yet here I am, nervous about how I look today...

Here I am, worried about so many "things" in my life. Here I am, regretting the choices I made yesterday. Here I am feeling low, and small, and vulnerable. How is this possible? If my story really is so cosmic, so unique, and so special—why do I feel so inadequate or unfulfilled? Why do I feel out of place? Why do I get upset and feel lonely, as if life isn't what it's supposed to be right now?

This book is an exploration of this theme, offering hope, and a few inspiring answers to these important questions.

CHAPTER 2

BREAKING THE CHAINS OF SELF DIVISION

The droning and groaning of all the cities on Earth

Entered my dream and quelled the living music

Rising from my heart.

I woke feeling unsure of my reality,

Fumbling nervously through make-believe-life,

Longing for the warmth of my own real sun....

Wishing for a ticket back home —

And I had forgotten where that is,

Until I looked with new eyes at the sun,

The real one, inside.

Our modern society suffers from a kind of chronic mental-emotional hang up. We might call it self-division, self-deception, or even self-sabotage. It is really just a shared misunderstanding, and once we see it for what it is, we can free ourselves from its stranglehold.

I see so many of my good friends and people that I know who are suffering from this painful misunderstanding, almost like a kind of forgetfulness.

Our modern global atmosphere is very much like a spiritual forgetfulness. It is a kind of tendency to move away from what we are, naturally, toward an imposed idea of what we are supposed to be. It has many symptoms. It manifests as a deep, almost fundamental feeling that there's something wrong with us.

It is so submerged, so deeply tangled up in our subconscious, that it is hard to put into words and we feel it more in the body than in the brain. Have you noticed how many people walk around stiffly, with a tense look on their faces, and such a protective, defensive body language? There are so few friendly greetings and warm hugs—especially in our big cities.

It feels like permanent tension, as if there is a barrier between the real world and us; as if there is some kind of invisible wall between a place of simple, natural ease, and where we actually find ourselves. It is a condition of the mind that closes the heart like a fist, and it makes us tough on the outside and cold on the inside.

Because all things are connected, and because subtle energy waves spread through resonance, these tense vibrations in the world can affect our individual minds and emotions.

It is as if we are living in a cloud of influence and the world-mind affects the way we feel about ourselves. We feel the disconnect. We start to think the same way that other people think: "Why do I feel incomplete? Why am I so tense and reactive? Why this constant resistance?"

We're not sure exactly what our defect is, but we feel it in our bones, in the pits of our stomachs as a knot of tension. It collects along our spines in tense muscle groups that never relax. It drives us a little crazy and it makes us more than a little neurotic.

"Life is hard, and unfair," so many of us tell each other. People nod and agree. "Yes, life is hard, and full of obstacles," they confirm and so a great crowd of us, we human wonders, we go about our business… We rush off, headlong, who knows where.

We are trying to make ends meet but the rope doesn't seem long enough. We are chasing a horizon but the boundary keeps receding.

But is it true? Is it meant to be this way? Am I supposed to struggle so hard to become... to become... what, exactly? Is there more to life than this?

It is a basic mistrust of living and existing.

The root cause of this discontent is a fundamental disconnect between the mind and the body; between who we think we are, who we imagine we are supposed to become, and the simple, child-like magic of raw nature.

We have simply forgotten who we are, at root. We have misplaced our innocent, barefoot joy of being.

On one level, it appears in society as a sense of alienation. As a collective human group, we feel unreal. There is something fictitious about the way we live. Look at our convenient, consumer-oriented way of living. Our culture has cut itself off from nature, from simplicity, from the real.

We can see it as humanity spreads across the globe, cutting and chopping its way through the green. We see it in crowds, where people ignore one another, glued to their phones. We can see it from the International space station, when darkness covers half the globe, and artificial lights almost entirely cover the surface of the continents.

We can see this theme in our movies and our literature, with stories about misfits and outsiders, people who deeply feel that they don't belong, as if something is amiss, like the hero of the Truman Show. We find this theme hidden in stories of humanity's desire for conquest, forgetting the miracle of the living world. We see it in stories about the end of the world, stories that tell us we're living in some kind of a dream, a sort of simulation, or a matrix, and stories that reveal a kind of world-feeling of doom.

It's the feeling that humanity is broken to the point of no repair. Why do we tell these stories? What secret are we trying to tell ourselves? What does the world-mind suspect that it cannot admit?

We have created a fictitious utopia in our minds, and it doesn't agree with the reality under our feet, so we feel discontented. We feel fear. We sense a collective hopelessness and disillusionment around us.

The same dis-ease manifests on another level within individuals. This world-feeling touches us individually, and it makes us feel as if we're broken, or somehow corrupted, as if we need a "ME" Version 2.0.

CHAPTER 3

WELCOMING HARMONY: TRUSTING THE FLOW OF LIFE'S JOURNEY

In so many of us, this same theme comes out as a feeling that are not enough in some way. So many of us feel chronically guilty for not being "more". So many of us feel unworthy of love. We want to reinvent ourselves, but we're not sure how to do that.

It's the feeling of: "I'm not good enough, and I don't measure up to the social standards. I don't seem to fit in, and I will never be like them." We might feel a sense of hopelessness. It is so easy to fall into self-doubt and the comparison game. Comparing yourself to the influencers of today, acquaintances, your coworkers, your friends, other moms; the list is endless.

It can happen to us when we least expect it, our world feels dark, even if we are normally quite resilient and balanced. Something happens in our lives, something unexpected, something we didn't want, plan or prepare for, and it divides us inwardly.

It might be a relationship that isn't what we thought it was, whether that a friend or romantic relationship. It might be struggling with infertility or having your idea of motherhood flipped upside down with your first newborn. It might happen while we go through a divorce, or when we face a challenge beyond our ability to cope in our career, or life might simply become too heavy, too full of complications.

Some of my best friends are going through challenges like these, and I would like to remind them that life is not all about heartache. Some of you are doubting yourselves and feeling as if life is passing you by. Some of you are in so much pain right now and I can understand where you are on your journey. Life can be heavy and sometimes it feels impossible to escape the sinking ship.

We are doing our best to take care of so many details, chores, responsibilities, meeting expectations, and barely making it through. Then life gives us one more disappointment, one more negative, one more way to take away our peace. We start getting negative feedback from our life situation, and we start to think, "Why do these things always happen to ME?"

No matter how hard I try, how sincerely I strive,

The goal seems further away now than it did before.

When will I arrive? When will I be perfect? When will I come into myself?

When will I be worthy of the love that I can sense, just there, over the horizon?

It seems the game will be over before I even learn how to play...

It can help us to transcend our life challenges if we understand what is happening. My mother was such an inspiration in this regard: She always pointed out the lessons and purpose of letdown and heartache. It is meant to ignite a kind of soul-search within us, so we can find out who we really are and be surprised at our own strength.

The poem above is the miserable song of the ego. Its refrain echoes in the lives of unhappy people all over the globe. I have heard that sad melody in my own heart too.

Some lucky and highly motivated people have escaped from this trap, to some degree, but others feel it, bone deep, almost all the time. Some of us feel as if we're not where we are supposed to be, we're not doing what we are meant to be doing in this life.

No matter what you are going through right now, no matter what your challenges were in the past, please know that there is nothing fundamentally wrong with you. Just as you made it through your difficulties before, so you will get through this one too.

Your circumstances don't define you. Recognize your core strength of heart. Recognize your own wisdom, no matter how small it may seem right now.

When last did you recognize your own strength, your own resilience, your own ability to make it through a dark place? Please remember that too, even as you encounter this feeling of hopelessness and self-criticism.

See it for what it is. The self-speak that corrodes us inside is not essentially us! It is a dialogue made of words and ideas. It is the way we are trying to understand ourselves and overcome our limits.

This sad lament of disconnect is just the unending quest of the personality. Its goal is to find itself, to perfect itself, to create itself out of nothing, and to live up to an impossible list of expectations. It is the relentless pursuit of sham self-improvement at the cost of the authentic natural beauty that we already possess.

The truth is that it's all a big misunderstanding.

Deep down, we are actually enjoying the process of life, which means constant reinvention and resilience. We love to rediscover our true inner beauty, courage and our strengths.

There's nothing by which we can measure the worth of a soul. We cannot judge or measure our being. There's nothing fundamentally wrong with us or with our life. The trouble arises in our heads when we buy into the stories we spin between our ears. We spend the currency of emotional energy when we buy into the stories we tell ourselves about ourselves.

The ego, as we use the word here, means the sense of "me" that we feel we have to manufacture and manipulate from the time we learn how to think. It is forever incomplete, forever vulnerable, forever discontent.

The true self, that from which we naturally and spontaneously arise, is always becoming, always disappearing, and happy to flow in that state. It is content to be born, to grow old, and to pass on, admiring the wonderful show, all the way through.

Look at children. Aren't they complete and perfect just as they are? There are no airs and graces about them. There is very little neurosis in our kids, at least, not yet. They are egoically naked and unashamed, in a sense.

There is no deep sense of guilt and unworthiness. They don't try to be what they are not. There are no false pretenses (except of course when they playfully pretend to be dragons or magic princesses!) They are just as they are and each child has their own quirks and peculiarities, but there is nothing fake about them.

Yes, it may be true that they have yet to grow into their full potential—but is that a defect? Isn't becoming and unbecoming simply the nature of life? Isn't the process of learning things anew, starting fresh with a blank slate, and becoming something completely unique, while discarding the outgrown, the whole point of the show?

The reality is that you were born whole, and natural, and right. I can see this in my daughters, and I am sure that every parent feels it too.

We can add very little to what we already are. The events that led to our existence are so ancient, so complex, and so beautiful and extraordinary that we cannot imagine the totality of it. Our parents didn't engineer us. They didn't design us on computer software and print us out in 3D. Their parents didn't carve them out of stone in a workshop somewhere—our ancestors, and the planet earth are not mistakes made by some careless clerk in a big office somewhere.

You are not a mistake. You are not defective. You are not incomplete. The great thing is that you are allowed to reinvent yourself as often as you like!

Our cosmos and the life on this planet were shaped by forces that modern science still struggles to understand. The spontaneous dance of eternity has led to who we are, how we are, and where we are...

All we have to do is embrace our natural uniqueness. All we have to do is surrender and relax, as we trust the process of living. We can't unfold into what we are becoming if we close our hearts like a fist. We must graciously let go of what we were in order to become what we are becoming.

But the world disagrees. "You have to make it. Fake it until you make it! You have to pass this grade before you reach the next... and the next.... and don't forget, you have to be a doctor, lawyer or have a traditional career to be successful. You have to force it. You have to will it. You have to achieve it or you're lazy and unmotivated. Put on a brave face. Wear an actor's mask, so we know which role you are playing, for heaven's sake!"

So the media, the collective face of the world, insists, but everyone fails and everyone falls short; yet there is no shortage of critics, and, sadly, there is a great shortage of compassion.

We end up playing a game of comparisons, and our minds like to cling to the negative comparisons more than the positive comparisons.

"This kind of bad thing always happens to me, and never to anybody else!" We say to ourselves.

"Everyone else is getting ahead in life—but here I am, stuck on the first stage!" We tell ourselves.

"I'm just not motivated enough. Other moms are staying fit, getting beauty treatments, running successful businesses while looking after their kids —but here I am, failing at all those things, I can't even put the laundry away!"

"Look at that happy couple. They have been married for twenty years and they have such respect for each other. What am I doing wrong? Why did I have to end up with this partner? Why can't I find true love?"

We tend to view ourselves in a negative light, forgetting that all those other people face challenges and problems too. Their lives really are not as perfect as we think they are.

Even more common, this feeling that "I'm not good enough" can be traced back to our early childhood.

No matter our background, our spirits can be injured in one way or another as children. Little children are incredibly sensitive, especially while we are trying on different personas, trying to figure out who we are and what we're worth. Teenagers are particularly vulnerable to this injury.

Right from our early formative years, around the time we go to school, we start learning that we have to put on a pretend face. We have to conform and the rebels have a tough time of it. We have to fit into society, the family, the school environment. We start trying to become someone special, someone respected, someone loved and admired, someone who fits in—someone "worthy" of love. If we do not conform, we are made to feel awful about it, so we try hard to please the world.

We have no idea how to do this, so we copy our role models and we try on different personas—but none of those tricks can ever reach our true inner nature, for that is something timeless, something untouched by ego.

This game of masks is the false persona, the idea of having to "become" who you are through some kind of program. The aim is to manipulate, to use, and to arrive, so people know your name. It is a dangerous game. It is one of the chief reasons we feel that we don't measure up.

At some point as we grow up, a seemingly harmless insult hits us and it goes in deep, like a knife into our spiritual-emotional-mental flesh.

It shapes a piece of our world-view, and it shapes the ego, the way we think about ourselves. The ego is vulnerable, because it is based on nothing substantial. We have to constantly protect and nurture the ego, and that makes us very tense inside. It is a never-ending chore.

Think back to those events that scarred your personality as a child. Why does it hurt so much when someone attacks our sense of self?

"You're a moron," some bully says and it hits home. Maybe it's true, we secretly think to ourselves. "You're so ugly," some mean person tells us in spite and the wound cuts deep. We fight back, we lash out with hurtful words of our own, but somewhere deep inside we wonder, "What if it's true? After all, there is something in me that feels unfinished and imperfect…"

Our bones remember. Our cells keep a record. A little scar remains—for years. We won't admit it, but it's there, and it still hurts, and it still makes us afraid in unconscious ways. "Why was I born this way…?"

Most human beings are resilient enough to fend off a few such attacks on the psyche, but children are not always so strong and, if they grow up in a loveless environment or without nurturing and affirmation—without balance—then those wounds can cut very deep indeed. They can stay with us for a lifetime.

Children are natural empaths. They are sensitive, delicate flowers, and they don't know how to set boundaries. A feeling of worthlessness can enter the heart of a child and remain until adulthood—and it happens far more often than we like to admit.

All of us have this experience in one way or another. It's part of growing up and we can't lay all the blame on other people. Each of us has to learn to protect, understand, and live with our inner sense of self—and this is such a delicate balance that it's almost like an art.

The key to self-healing from this world malady is to realize what is happening inside us and to see it for what it is.

We can't unfold into what we are becoming

if we close our hearts like a fist.

CHAPTER 4

LOVE'S UNVEILING: SEEKING BELONGING AND HAPPINESS WITHIN

What we are really searching for is closer than our own skin,

Closer than our own mind,

Closer even than the tangled nests of love woven in our own hearts...

My deepest desire is to be loved, to be accepted, to be treasured for who I am, so I can be happy. I believe that this same feeling exists within the heart of every human being. It's what drives us, ultimately.

Why do all living things want to survive? Because we love to live, and live to love. Surviving makes us happy, happiness helps us survive. The universe delights in living. We might say that the universe loves to create and what she creates, at least here on this planet, is an abundance of life.

Why do we make friends? Is friendship not a kind of love? The universe hangs together by means of shared energy, which is another name for love. Why do we need family? Why do we pursue romantic love? Why do we crave recognition and acceptance, and strive to feel as if we belong? These are all subtle differences in the various aspects of one need: Love.

Love is at the root of almost everything we do, provided we dig deeply enough to discover our ultimate motives. Admittedly, part of our motivation involves avoiding pain—but why do we avoid pain? Is it not because we love ourselves enough to look after ourselves? We love to protect what we love. These are merely opposite sides of one coin, opposite ends of one stick. The one end, seeking happiness, is positive and the other end, avoiding pain, is negative—but it's essentially the same motive.

All our lives we are chasing that feeling of happiness, looking to find it outside our own skins.

When we are little children, we look for it in our parents. It takes time to cut the apron strings. Why? We crave that love, that nurturing, that womb of protection and belonging. If we feel that our parents do not love us, our world shatters into pieces.

We look for a form of love and belonging from our brothers and sisters. Why do we love to fight so much with each other? Why do we stick up for each other, no matter what? Why do we say, "Blood is thicker than water?" It's that same universal love—just in another form.

We look for a different form of that same feeling of love in our friends at school. If we are lucky, we find friendships that last for a lifetime and feel like soulmates.

We must have been stars that orbited each other

When the universe was a child,

Or we washed up on the shore together like two halves of the same shell,

For our friendship feels as ancient as the night sky,

As deep as the ocean,

And our meeting seems fated by a power

That keeps us entangled in support and understanding.

Later, we yearn for the same love, but now in a completely different way. We look for it in our first love affairs. Now it becomes deeply personal and very powerful.

The English language has only one word to describe these energies of bonding—"love." Other languages are richer in this regard. Ancient Greek used a number of words to describe aspects of love, including philia (affectionate love), pragma (mature, enduring love), storge (family love), eros (romantic love), and agape (selfless love). There are more besides these. There is even a word for self-love, namely, philautia. Roughly translated, that means self-esteem, in the positive sense, and hubris or narcissism in the negative.

"Love" takes many forms. It takes the shape of every bond in the universe.

We crave love from our children and, one day, from our grandchildren. We want to love our jobs, we want other people to acknowledge and respect us, and we want to feel the love and joy that success in life brings…

The feeling of love has one taste, one texture, one basic fabric, although it has many different outward forms. We search for this feeling of love and acceptance everywhere, seldom suspecting that it's right here, in the middle of us.

It's waiting here, to be seen, acknowledged, to be known, to be expressed and radiated, sun-like, outward, back out into the big world around us, the world filled with all those people and things—the big unfriendly world—the very place where we are searching for love. But it's not out there. That's not its real source, that's not its home. What we find out there are shadows and reflections, dappled and diffused through other beings. The love from another helps for a while, but it doesn't ultimately satisfy our deepest urge, because we are seeking the source.

We can't earn love, we can't deserve it, we can't manufacture it, we can't live up to it—because we are love. It's the source of us, as we are the source of it.

Why can't I find love in the world around me? Is there something wrong with me?

No, there's nothing wrong with me, it's simply because I have cut myself off from self-love. The real thing, the true source, is here, within me.

If the one who is seeking love does not trust the love in his or her own heart, then love cannot be mirrored in the outside world. To know love is to know the self. To know the self is to know love.

We mirror our self-love out into the world. If we love and accept ourselves, we love and accept others. If we judge and criticize others, we judge and criticize ourselves, and vice versa. If we hate ourselves, we cannot accept that others can love us as we are. The opposite poles of love are woven together as one.

This natural insight can free us from trying to be... to become... to fight to become...something we are not.

People who are complete narcissists often behave the way they do because, deep down, they feel a lack of true self-love, so they overcompensate. Those who are compulsive people-pleasers suffer from the same affliction, but express it in the opposite way—the energy flows in the other direction. At root, both of these types suffer from a lack of true self-acceptance and self-love.

We can redirect our love, our energy, our minds, our willpower to who we truly are, underneath all the layers of social masks. To love ourselves, we do not have to be polite, nice, likable, and we don't have to be people-pleasers. We do not have to be achievers, influencers, or celebrities—we don't have to look perfect. To love ourselves, we need to embrace ourselves just as we are, for what we are, deep down—our essence. We need to really embrace the feeling of just being. The silent, ever-present, self-existing core of me, the one that watches through my eyes, the one that sees my thoughts, my feelings, my emotions —that is the home of love.

Deep down, on a fundamental level—how do you value yourself?

CHAPTER 5

BEYOND MEASURE: DISCOVERING INTRINSIC WORTH AND AUTHENTIC VALUE

Can I be worth more than the sky, the mountains, the ocean, or less?

Am I worth more than the tiniest birds in the trees, or less?

Am I worth-thee, or worth-less?

Am I worth the trouble I caused my parents?

And, if so, are my children worth the trouble they cause me?

Is a life lived as me

worth the price?

When we ask from the mind, we cannot be wholehearted;

When we answer from the heart, we don't need to think about it.

There are two ways to assign value. One way is to discriminate and to judge and weigh the differences between things in our minds. The other way is to feel the essential quality of something in our hearts.

The two ways do not always agree with one another. Our hearts and our minds can rub up against each other like fire sticks, creating friction. The head wants one thing, but the heart wants another. This is true when it comes to finding our own true worth as well. For example, weigh the following questions in your mind and then in your heart.

Do you feel that you are worth more than your neighbor or less? What about your partner, or your boss, or a random homeless person, someone drunk, down and out on the street? Who is worth more? How do we judge the worth of somebody?

These questions do not really mean all that much, from a wide-lens perspective, and yet we subconsciously ask this basic question all the time. We're constantly judging ourselves, weighing our worth, our value, and our relative importance. We gauge our value by comparing ourselves to others. The rules of the "value" game keep shifting, though. The top dog in one yard may well be the underdog in another yard. If we are important in one group, we may well be sideliners in another group of people.

If we don't use a number, like a dollar value or an IQ, then how can we figure out what we are worth?

To see the truth of our being is to see value. In other words, when we use the heart, when we appreciate that which is already here. Our minds will go on judging value indefinitely, but that is of little consequence.

Our real value belongs to something that is difficult to name. It belongs to that which is aware in us, that which is alive in us. We see value and beauty and wonder when we look out at the world from that fathomless place, the way a child looks at the world.

This conscious act, this way of looking, in the spirit of love, completely dissolves the question of worth.

We can live our lives from our minds, stuck in our heads, judging things—or—we can live our lives from the heart; in other words, from a place of accepting love. It's a choice we each have to make. Where will I create my center of gravity? The head or the heart?

Love embraces all things equally because it understands that all things are one. We cannot exist without our environment; our environment cannot exist without us. Our existence, the strange story of an entire lifetime, is a flowing transaction between environment and self.

If we value the inside—our source—then we naturally love and value the outside, or the "other." It's one thing. Inside and outside exist in a living interaction. What goes on inside affects what happens outside, and vice versa.

Our circumstances can be awful or they can be wonderful, depending on the "goggles" we have over our eyes. When our inner energy is low, life seems more difficult and painful. When we have an abundance of energy, everything seems more pleasant. We are the ones who create the differences.

Why do we experience feelings of unworthiness? Why is it that we can secretly run the following kind of inner dialogue in our heads and hearts:

"I feel unworthy of love. I have never known true love. How could they love me when I look/act like this?"

We find ourselves even resenting those who try to love us. Why?

It happens when we lose touch with our heart center and listen only to the voice in our heads. Our human orbit becomes wobbly because we don't have a steady center of gravity in our hearts. We're adrift in head space, gradually falling toward the wrong star.

Feelings of self-worth underpin so much of our life, and an unhealthy self-relationship undermines us in so many dimensions.

A deep self-examination forces us to confront the guilt, the shame, frailty, inexperience, weakness, and vulnerability. Am I not where I am supposed to be in life? Why can't I seem to get to where I want to be in my life? Why can I not become who I aspire to be? Is it true? Can it really, really be true?

If so, what does that say about the world around me? If I condemn my core, then I condemn the universe from which I am extruded because I grow out of the universe as a hair grows out of my head. If I condemn my inner core, then I condemn my whole body, my whole interaction with everything outside of myself. If I condemn myself, I condemn the universe too.

It helps tremendously to see a clear distinction here. Nobody created the core essence of what I am. The self-image, the persona, the mask that I create through life is temporary.

The universe is self-perpetuating, self-sustaining, and self-patterning. Just as an apple tree produces apples, so the planet Earth produces life forms and human beings are part of that marvelous biosphere. We arise from earth in due season, as cherries appear on cherry trees in due season, as clouds arise in the sky when the conditions are right. We are natural beings. Nature is us, as we interact with everything else. The universe, the planet, the human race found it worthwhile to produce—me. Each of us is a delicious, weird, colorful fruit of existence.

By distinction, the ego, the persona, the person we are trying to manufacture, through mind, willpower, and delusion, on top of this self-existent frame, is artificial.

If we hate the person we are, then what we are really criticizing is not the core self, not that which exists by itself, but the overlay. We don't like our moods, our mannerisms, our habits, our conditioning, or our programming. But we can change those things! We can re-engineer the veneer of our ego.

We can't change our essential being because it is perfect just as it is and, honestly, that is not the thing that bothers us. The things we don't like about ourselves are the things we have added to that, and that usually means the ego.

Befriend your ego. It's not you, essentially. It's your tool and your plaything. Shape it the way you like, trash it, and start over if you like. Do with your ego what you will, for it can never replace you, it can never truly usurp the throne of self. The ego is a wonderful ally, a good servant, but a terrible master.

The true self can never be injured. The ego is like a bullseye for pain. Think of it this way: Why does it hurt when we are insulted?

"You're too sensitive… You're naïve… You're being childish… "Why does it feel true? Why does it push our buttons?

Because we don't know ourselves deeply, and we mistake the content (our thoughts and feelings, our programming and education) for the essence. We identify with a story and the plot of the story is "I'm not good enough." We forget that it's just a story.

This is a big reason why something like social media can potentially be poison for our self-relationship. We constantly compare ourselves to something imaginary, forgetting the real thing, here inside our own skin.

The world-mind has lost its master standard by which it measures human value. There's an interesting story that illustrates this. In October 1834, the United Kingdom Houses of Parliament were destroyed in a fire. Among the items lost were the objects that defined the imperial standards of length and mass. These were objects that had very specific weights, like exactly one imperial pound or a metal rod that had a length of precisely one imperial yard, for instance. It was a bit of a disaster. A new copy for each unit of measure had to be made, and later this "master yardstick" was sent over to the U.S. so we could have a standard with which to measure lengths.

But did any of those master measurements make even the slightest difference to any real thing in nature? Or was it simply a crisis of the human mind?

There is no such golden yardstick by which we can measure our worth, but that doesn't stop the world from measuring us anyway. People have replaced the yardstick of the heart with a copy in the head, based on the ego, and it doesn't measure up.

Look at how most people tend to define their worth. They measure it by the kind of person who agrees to be in a relationship with them. They measure worth by their family name, their gender, their race, how much money they have at their disposal, their power to influence or control other people, their social position, the recognition they get, the number of "likes" on social media...

None of these things can be our yardstick for measuring what we are worth.

No, there's nothing wrong with us.

We have simply forgotten who we really are, and what that is actually worth.

You are worth so much that the entire universe conspired to tell your story.

Strip away the veil of ideas and definitions, and we are left with a great mystery.

The dance of life doesn't ask any creature whether it is worthy—only we humans injure ourselves in this way.

CHAPTER 6

THE PARADOX OF SELF-DEFINITION AND CONNECTION

Failure does not define me,

Loss cannot limit me,

Rejection can never box me in,

The opinions of others can never cage my worth,

For my spirit is so big, so boundless in energy,

My mind's horizons so vast,

My heart so big,

That my own body can barely contain me for the span of a lifetime.

How do you *define* yourself?

"Define" is an interesting word in the English language. It probably comes from the Latin *definire*, which means "to limit, determine, or explain." The root idea is that a definition rips something out of the infinite, out of all things, and crunches it down into a finite, understandable size.

Our minds have this power. We do this so that we can see an object clearly and understand exactly what it is. We want to see how it relates to everything around it. To do this, we cut it out and set clear limits. Definitions are, by their very nature, limiting.

Think about it. What are your limits? What makes you stand out as different and unique from the totality of all things in the infinity of the cosmos? What are the things that are essentially you? What things are you not? Where do you begin, and where do you end?

Now think about things that join you as one with everything around you, so there is no clear dividing line. For instance, think of your breath, your eyesight, all your senses, and your language. These things are in you, but they link you to everything around you. They simultaneously limit you and set you free.

Is it your skin that separates you from everything or does it join you to everything? Both ways of looking at it are true, in their own way. Not so?

The things you do and say may set you apart as an individual but the things you do and say are also interactions with everything else. They join, link, and relate you to everything as much as they separate you as an individual.

In one sense, you are limited. In another very important sense, just as valid and just as meaningful, you are limitless. "You" are so much bigger and richer than just a body, just a list of behaviors.

The truth is that your definition is what you believe you are. It has no meaning outside of your own way of thinking. It is just an idea and you are so much more than an idea.

Your definition can become your self-imposed limit. It may be a limit that society imposes on you, true enough, but you agree to that limit, for good reasons or for no reason at all, and that agreement gives power to that limit.

The things that you believe about yourself will start to become your reality. What you think you are is the destiny you are creating for yourself.

If you believe that you are the hero of the story, that's the way you will act. If you believe that you are the villain in the story, that's the way you act instead. If you see yourself as a victim, that's what you will live. If you see yourself as overcoming impossible odds, that becomes real for you instead.

If you believe you are doomed to fail, chances are very good that you will fail. If you believe in your heart that you can break that record, smash that boundary, overcome that challenge, or make that positive leap, chances are you will succeed. You may fail many times, but each time you will learn and one day you will make it.

Everyone who has done something unbelievable, something amazing, something that others find impossible, believed in themselves enough to break the limits of their definitions. They trusted their essential power more than they believed in their limits.

I bet you have done something unbelievable too. I bet that you haven't even acknowledged or realized how incredible it was. Be proud of that. Wear that as your badge of honor. You have made many strides through the darkness, you've figured it out along the way, and you are still smiling. You have shown up in the world with grace and humility when you didn't need to. And there are countless other things that you have forgotten, but all of them are amazing.

This truth of life goes right to the core of what we are. I would like to ask you this: What is your essence?

It may seem like a simple question, but really, if we want a good answer, this is one of the deepest philosophical and spiritual questions of all time.

Who am I? What am I?

The more deeply we probe this question, the more perplexingly unsatisfied we are with our answers.

The truth is that the things we use to define—or to limit—ourselves are often quite arbitrary. For example, we might say, "I am a female," or we might say, "I am a male." (In this case, it's taken for granted that we're human.)

We use specific words like "university graduate," "mother," or our job title to define who we are, versus what we are not.

In reality, these words don't explain us and they don't truly limit us. They are partial descriptions of our attributes or qualities, for now. They don't explain our essential nature.

Essentially

I am not my likes and dislikes,

I am not my history of choices,

I am not my body, for my body is forever changing, yet I'm still here,

I am not my nationality, my race, my gender, or my eye color,

I am not defined by my name, my lineage, my ancestral history, my tribe,

I am not my neuroses, my hang-ups, my habits, my failings,

I am not the things that I lack,

I am not the accolades and merits that I may or may not achieve,

For all these things are like the changing weather,

But I remain,

containing them all, yet untouched by them,

as the vast blue sky.

The words are only vague descriptions. Our minds find these words useful to identify ourselves in the confusing abundance of things around us. The mind finds it difficult to process an answer like "I am a piece of everything," or "I am a mystery."

"That may well be true," argues the mind, "but what does it mean? How on earth do I use that information?"

Dear mind... dear obsessive, chattering mind...

When we see something that fills us with awe—the starry night sky, a piece of nature, a beautiful, wise human being—are we thinking about how we can use it? Value does not mean the same as utility or usefulness.

That which I love is not an object to be used. I love it for what it is.

The mind gets caught, ensnared, and hypnotized by words and their definitions. Our rational faculty is trying to use words to find the truth about a living, flowing, ever-changing truth, but this is impossible.

The result is that we get ourselves into a tangled mess, because we fully believe in the labels that are assigned to us.

"You're so clever," somebody compliments us and the mind finally has a label to hang on the self. "I am clever! Who knew? How nice." We start wearing a "clever" personality.

"You're just not talented at singing," somebody informs us and it becomes a defining limit in our lives forever. "Mathematics is not my strong suit," we tell our parents and the label sticks for a lifetime.

Our definitions limit us. They keep us trapped in cages of words and ideas. They often tend to focus on what we lack, rather than what makes us unique. The definitions completely ignore that which is universally human, because we all share it. (Things like having a heart, or an imagination, are not considered "special" or "unique.")

We reinforce those limiting mental cages with the stories we constantly spin in our heads. Those stories are made by using words, which have definitions.

What would happen if we dropped all our self-definitions?

Would we disappear? Would we stop living? Would we melt into the universe around us, as if we had never existed?

Or would we become free? Wouldn't it feel like we had a giant weight lifted from our shoulders? For a heart filled with love and acceptance, compassion and joy, no definition can become a cage.

The heart is not bound by definitions the way the mind is bound by them. The heart can accept infinity, chaos, and confusion, just as it is, and still have the capacity to appreciate the finite—the individual, single being, as it rests in perfect harmony with all "other" things. Why? Because to the heart that is pure, there is no real "other."

Just as the difference between a "rock" and a "stone" is important in some ways, but essentially just a matter of relative size and how we choose to name things, so the difference between "me" and "not me" is really a matter of relativity. It depends on how we want to look at it.

Understanding this clearly can help us to free ourselves from limiting negative beliefs about ourselves.

So often, failure defines a person's life path. We get stuck on what could have been, what should have been, instead of what IS.

Too often, our circumstances define us, limit us, and box us in. We imagine that our bank balance, our job title, our relationship status, our skill at cooking, our address, or our outfit defines us in some way. We imagine our success or failure at relationships defines us.

What really is—right here now—is so much better than we think. Remove the idea that" this is not good enough", and suddenly the world shines with a new light.

We wrap our worth around the delicate threads of external validation, allowing limiting beliefs to construct the walls that confine us.

Yet, in the depths of our being there lies a truth waiting to be unearthed. It whispers softly, reminding us that what really is—right here, right now—is so much more magnificent than our minds can fathom.

It beckons us to release the heavy burden of inadequacy, to let go of the notion that we are not good enough. With every layer shed, the world unfolds before us, revealing a kaleidoscope of possibilities.

Embrace this transformative realization, for you are a masterpiece in progress, an ever-evolving wonder of resilience and strength. Break free from the chains of self-doubt and shine your light with unwavering brilliance.

Embrace your true essence, for within it lies the power to redefine yourself beyond the confines of limiting beliefs. Trust the infinite potential that resides within and let it guide you toward a life of authenticity and fulfillment. You are a radiant soul, destined to create a symphony of your own design.

Perfection is not a prerequisite for life, for happiness, or for self-worth.

Love accepts imperfection. In fact, real love is what celebrates imperfection.

If all the human beings that have ever lived, and all those who are still to be born, could be combined into one human being—would that be perfection? Would that perfection not include every "imperfection" of every human too?

Nature is perfectly imperfect. Streams and rivers do not follow perfectly straight lines, they curve and sway with the landscape, landscaping as they go. Trees that grow in nature do not grow perfectly straight to provide perfectly straight beams for our perfectly square homes. They are gnarled, and twisting, and bent, and perfectly wonderful. Clouds in the sky do not appear as perfect sugar cubes, at least, not as a rule. They come out perfectly unique and they change all the time.

Nature does not give us the impression that it is striving to live up to some kind of definition. We sense, instead, that nature is spontaneously, effortlessly becoming what it is, playing with new ways to express a gorgeous, harmonious pattern. That overall symmetry includes all kinds of things that we think of as "imperfections." It includes yellowing leaves, wilting flowers, broken branches, and bugs that live off decay. Are those "imperfections?" Or do all those imperfections combine into a perfect environment for life?

Are we any different? What are our human standards of "perfection" compared to the marvel, the strange living potential, the weird spontaneous creativity, that we already are.

Why not relax into that?

You are self healing, self-sufficient, self-aware and self-sustaining.

Everything you need is already in you, with you, all around,

And deep inside, waiting to be expressed in your story.

CHAPTER 7

RELEASE AND RENEWAL: (RE)BUILDING YOURSELF

When my world shattered,

What lay in shards at my feet

Were only my illusions about me,

not my true nature.

When my world broke, only my shell broke open,

never injuring my real spirit, the real me, which was hatching for the first time.

When my heavy world all fell away from me, my burden felt lighter.

When I finally lost my whole world, I finally gained myself,

only to realize,

There is nothing to shatter, nothing to break, nothing to lose. The world keeps on changing, but I remain, watching.

A friend told the following story: A few years ago, a forest fire ravaged the area where he lives. It was red and orange chaos, with searing heat and columns of flame roaring higher than the rooftops. People had to evacuate their homes. Forest critters fled in all directions, panicking, trying desperately to escape the heat and smoke. It was heartbreaking.

Afterward the landscape was blackened and charred. Smoke continued to rise from the scorched earth for days. It looked ghostly, almost apocalyptic, and it felt like the end of the world. The electricity went out, so the nights were inky black and it really felt like a dark night of the soul.

It took a few months, but the rain fell. And one day, in the middle of that black and gray wasteland, the first green shoots sprouted out between the layers of ash. He told me that the first delicate little plant that he noticed was so incredibly green! He couldn't believe anything could be so luminous, and so alive.

It was so beautiful, so brave, so hopeful that it thrilled his heart. A week later, thousands upon thousands of little green shoots of hope sprang up all around it and, do you know? It has been three or four years now, and you almost wouldn't suspect that a fire had ever raged in his homeland.

Almost everything has grown back and, if you ask him, the landscape looks even healthier than it did before. Here and there a few blackened snags still stand between the new green, as reminders of what happened, but they are getting harder to spot now. He tells me that this year the spring flowers were rampant, almost as if they were making up for lost time. The bees have all returned, and the birds are all nesting again. Homes have been repaired or rebuilt, and life goes on. Isn't that amazing?

Moral of the story: Nature is self-healing,

and so *are you.*

The same nameless magic that preserved that little seed of life in the midst of that inferno is within me too. I can sense it. That force, that unexplainable something that inspired nature to try again, to wake up, to be reborn, to sprout up, and struggle through the ash—that same magic is alive in you too.

Life can heal from anything; life will find a way.

In fact, it's happening to us all the time, but we hardly notice. While life is busy finding a way, through us, in us, and all around us, we are busy worrying about tomorrow or regretting yesterday. We're planning for security and dreaming of a paradise, but life keeps on doing its thing all the while, finding a way, despite our plans, despite our dreams.

We're constantly self-repairing. We are constantly recreating our cells, our muscles, and the thoughts in our heads, reshaping our worldviews. We hardly notice, but we're springing back to life each morning, each moment, and it happens spontaneously, despite our big plans.

We don't need to explain exactly how our skin heals from a bruise or a cut before the healing happens. Our physical systems naturally want to fight off infection and resist illness. We don't have to worry about making our hearts beat and we don't even have to think about breathing.

Our bodies always try to maintain homeostasis—balance. Do we have to give our cells instructions, do we have to police their work, or nag or beg them to comply? No, of course not! The body takes care of healing on its own. Our bodies have a natural intelligence. With just a little help and care, and provided we don't totally abuse them, our bodies last for a lifetime, more or less.

We're equipped to heal spontaneously, although we're not meant to last forever in this individual shape. While our life force inhabits this body, a dynamic intelligence takes care of mending all kinds of "broken" things and it does it all the time without needing our mental instructions.

In fact, our minds can get in the way of healing. Our constantly struggling egos can make us so tense that we take a long time to heal. Our own self-division can make us keep injuring ourselves instead of falling back into the natural.

If we keep telling ourselves that our spirits are broken, our bodies listen, and hear the message, and respond accordingly...

If we look very closely at what is going on, we can discover that the thing that is making us so unhappy is exactly this: Our attempt to make ourselves happy. The attempt, the will, the coercing to change things, to change ourselves, to fight and struggle in a tense and forceful way to get where we believe we ought to be—that is the whole cause of our sense of suffering.

But it doesn't *have* to be that way.

Just like our bodies, our emotions and our minds also have self-healing powers. A broken heart can mend. A disturbed mind can find equilibrium again, given time, patience and the right environment. Our spirits are unbreakable.

We have a name for these miracle-healing powers: hope.

Hope has many friends, including acceptance, wisdom, peace, joy, and open-heartedness.

When our minds are balanced and our hearts at peace, we sleep well and heal quickly. We wake up with energy and we feel more than capable of grappling with life's challenges. In fact, we enjoy the challenges. We might even seek out a difficult problem, just for the hell of it, just so we can grow our creative powers and hone our skills.

A fool's hope is just fantasy, just wishful thinking; but real hope, the healing kind, is different. It is rooted in reality. It comes from a keen observation of nature, not from daydreams or ego games.

Real hope arises from real wisdom. Wisdom comes through resilience. Resilience comes from experience. Experience happens when we engage with life fearlessly and with our whole being.

An accepting heart, one that says "Yes" to the moment, has a transformative power. It changes any circumstance into gold. We may not like it, we may not approve, but if we say yes, internally, we can work with living reality instead of just the veneer of theory and mind-stuff.

When we say "Yes" inside us, accepting all things just as they are, then we stop resisting. That surrender frees up a reservoir of creative, healing energy. The energy is no longer being squandered on pointless resistance, so it flows naturally to where it is needed for regrowth, rebirth, and regeneration.

That doesn't mean we give up. It means we stop struggling against our essential nature and cooperate instead. We engage in a new way with exactly the same circumstances and suddenly things begin to change because we have changed inwardly.

Things happen in life that can make us feel broken and burned to the ground. It's almost inevitable in this life to lose a loved one, to be disappointed in love, to fail at something, to struggle, to break something, or to make a big mistake somehow. When it happens, the last thing we want to do is engage fearlessly with life. Hope and all of hope's fine buddies seem far, far away.

When we break, it feels as if our inner world has been ravaged by fire and now all is black and gray, smoldering in ashes. But give it a few weeks, or months, and something new arises. Just wait and see—you won't believe how beautiful it is. Change the eyes that are looking at the circumstances, and the world shines again.

Nevertheless, you are *not* broken. You are experiencing a transformation and maybe the change is painful. It is happening so that something new, something living and luminous, can rise up from the ashes. This is not just a cliché, or a nice thing to say. It is the nature of life, of existence, to constantly change and flow into new places, new forms, new regions of mind, new revelations of truth. The old must burn away so the new can arise.

Things that no longer serve your truth, your wholehearted authenticity—these things must be shed and that can be painful. You have invested energy and time in those things. They were important, once. Letting go feels like a world burning down. The little old self protests, "No! You're not strong enough. You will break. You can't leave me here!"

But if we want to live, we must go on.

One part of us may still long to be a little child, free from responsibility. Another part of us wants to be grown up, whole, and mature. These two parts of us must find a way to manage the journey together—and a big part of accomplishing that is to let go, and let go, and let go of the past.

You are incredibly resilient, even though it might not feel that way right now.

The hero's journey is a name for the central plot development in most of the movies we love.

It may be an action movie, or a romantic comedy, but the hero—the main character—faces some kind of challenge. The protagonist has to overcome seemingly impossible difficulties to reach the goal. The goal may be to save the damsel in distress, to complete the quest, or to find happiness in love, but there is always an obstacle to that goal.

Without the obstacles, there is no story. "Hero saves world," or "girl meets boy and lives happily ever after" make for dull storylines. The fun is in the challenges, the plot twists, and the troubles. The way the hero fights and shows character, intelligence, guts, inventiveness, and resilience despite all the odds, heart, despite all the discouragement—those are the things that make the movie.

To wish that life stays the same forever, that life stays safe, and predictable, and "perfect," is to wish for a kind of paralysis. Life is unpredictable; life is messy, challenging, and painful sometimes for a good reason. It's supposed to be that way and we actually want it to be that way, or we could never become what we are. Our stories would be dull without our challenges.

We could never experience our depth of character, develop a backbone, or become strong without our troubles. We could never create anything new. We could never have a fresh experience. We could never see things with new eyes if the world was permanently frozen in "nice and neat."

If we have already solved all our problems and achieved every single goal, why live? What kind of a story would that be?

"You" are an experience that the universe is having. You are a unique aperture for consciousness. You are one unique way in which the universe gets to know what it is and what it could become in future.

Your bones may break. Your heart may break. Objects in the world around you may break. Your essence is that which sees the broken things and tries to mend what it can and let go of what it cannot.

You cannot actually break. You cannot be wrong, misshapen, incorrect, or unsuitable. You are an experience through you, in you, for you...

Whether you fail or succeed, you and your troubles are what make the story so interesting, so human, and so endearing. It doesn't really matter if you fail—and in fact, you can't fail, in the ultimate sense. You are allowed to start over and reinvent yourself as many times as you like. The story isn't over yet.

We don't mourn our skin cells that slough off from us in the shower. We don't need to mourn the shedding of an old self, a self that is always dying to be reborn, because it's happening for a reason—so we can grow in wisdom, in our capacity for love and acceptance, so we can continue fresh and unhindered by old habits, so we can evolve our awareness.

CHAPTER 8

REINVENTION, GROWTH, AND THE EVER-UNFOLDING SELF

Flowing, changing, rippling with the waves like a river song,

I am forever falling from the sky to the earth,

Forever arriving at the ocean,

Never finished, never the same, never standing still,

Always flowing, flowing home,

For my real home is the state of flow.

The living truth is that every moment expresses a "new you." The past is no longer available; it is not here anymore. This moment is a doorway, inviting you to bring your best, brand-new self to bear on the situation, whatever it may be.

This moment doesn't need to fit the expectations of yesterday, of parents, of friends, or even the expectations of your previous self. This moment is fresh, alive, and full of unknown potential. It doesn't need to copy the moment that came before. It wants to explore the New, and the Now.

We do not normally think of it as "reinvention," but all through life we are becoming something new. All through our lives we are dropping the old and saying goodbye to what was in order to greet what is.

We imagine that there is a continuation of the old because we recognize the face in the mirror and because we remember where we are, what people call us, and how we got here. That whole story exists in the mind and in memory. If we cling to yesterday, then yesterday binds us in chains. A big part of that story is conditioning—habits, fixed patterns. That story of yesterday makes us feel stuck, fixed, frozen somehow. It makes us feel worn out, like old shoes.

The lived, directly experienced truth is that we are more like ongoing processes of change than fixed things. This moment cannot be frozen because it is alive and it flows, and so do you.

First, we are these tiny babies, hardly conscious of the world around us—but that doesn't last long. We grow into something new. We feel that we are somehow both the same thing, and somehow different. We are growing. The process of life reinvents billions of cells in us, through us, and for us. We're composed of completely new "stuff" all the time, yet weirdly, we still feel like ourselves.

We do not remain in baby form forever. Soon we are staring wide-eyed at everything, absorbing sponge-like, growing, and reaching out. The changes come quickly in our first decade, and life seems to stretch out ahead forever. "Old age? It will never happen to me!"

Little children have a natural sense of awe. They are still in flow. They are malleable, like water. The simplest things can fascinate their eyes and hands and the simplest toys, weird details, colors, can bring such joy into their hearts.

By the time we're teenagers, we start to imagine that we know everything and that we've seen it all before, and our natural sense of awe is replaced by a kind of dissatisfaction. Mostly, we're dissatisfied with ourselves.

"When will my life finally begin? When can I become me and do what I want to do? I can't wait to get older!" A teenager thinks, forgetting that it is happening, right now.

The world hasn't become less interesting, less awe-inspiring; our minds and egos have only started to cover our eyes with a veil.

Even so, we are constantly flowing, like a river. Life never stands still and our world-view can keep on growing indefinitely. The more we learn, the more we discover how little we actually know. By the time we're old and gray, we have to admit that we hardly scratched the surface.

In a very important sense, you really have no other choice. You're going to reinvent yourself anyway.

Life is a master of the curve ball. Will you copy what you did yesterday, hoping to hold on to a pattern that works, more or less? Maybe that pattern is frustrating, and toxic. Are you going to take a risk and live?

Look around. Everything is brand-new when our eyes have the capacity to see it. All things change, whether they change instantly or take many centuries to change.

The one who is looking has already changed, simply by looking. The act of observing changes the thing that is observed and it changes the observer too—even though it may be in the subtlest ways.

The planet Earth, our beloved Gaia, is a creative soul. She reinvents her wardrobe every single day and she wears a new, dazzling starlit garment every night. Sometimes her mood is gray and rainy, sometimes she is sunny and bright, sometimes cold as ice, sometimes hot as a summer noonday. She loves variety, she loves color, and she adores diversity. She is never bored and she is never, ever boring!

You are a child of that same diversity. You come from her and you walk within her changes, changing as you go. You are reinvented every morning, so have no fear. Flow with her and dance with her moods.

"I don't feel creative!" you protest. Well, tell that to the 330 billion cells you created today. Tell that to the very next thought that pops into your head. Where did that thought come from?

All day long, you are creating energy, generating moods, causing emotional vibes, and lighting up thoughts upon thoughts upon thoughts, making plans, and living. To live is to be creative. To solve problems is to be inventive. To make it to the next day, we have to recreate ourselves one more time.

How do I reinvent myself? I honestly don't know, yet it is happening anyway and I am happy to flow with it.

I can tell you what holds me back. It's the idea of being "stuck." It is the belief in stickiness, it is the world-view that I'm somehow permanently fixed and stuck in a place I don't like. It's a story stuck in my head.

There is something automatic and compulsive inside me and it wants to live life on autopilot, repeating the same old patterns over and over again, no matter how toxic, negative, and painful they may be.

It is something like the fear of the unknown, the fear of floating free without a tether. It's as if I'm constantly telling myself: "If I don't have my pet pain, if I don't have my familiar troubles, if I don't have my constant companion, anxiety, won't I cease to exist completely? If I let go, I'm being naïve. If I let go, my world will unravel at the edges. I may be stuck, but at least I'm stuck somewhere familiar... better the devil you know...isn't that true? Don't venture out too far, you don't know what's out there."

The thing is, I only feel truly alive when I venture out into the new and discover, to my eternal surprise, that my clinging to "safe yesterday" was actually quite pointless.

What holds us back is procrastination, believing we don't have the ability, it's not the right time, or worrying about what other people will say. What holds us back is self-sabotage, reinforcing the self-speak that comes up with a thousand reasons why we can't flow with life.

The automatic, conditioned part of us—what we call the ego—is always afraid to take the leap. It is concerned with self-preservation and with saving face. It doesn't want to be seen making a mistake. It is what pretends to be a constant in our lives and it doesn't like to confront the fact that all things are temporary, that all things change. The idea of flow scares the life out of the ego, so it holds us prisoner, playing it safe, while life goes on reinventing itself all around us and we feel more acutely than ever that, somehow, we're being left behind.

Be like the universe. Have the courage to reinvent yourself every moment. It's happening anyway, so have no fear.

There's no need to start from scratch every time. You get to re-use the patterns that have worked well in the past but you are no longer bound by them. You get to put a fresh spin on everything. You get to use a new brush today, to try a new color or a new texture of sound, a new way of approaching life, even if that means tweaking one tiny detail.

This life is one big canvas and soon the canvas will be wiped clean again, so don't be afraid to splash some paint. Make that mistake; it might be the most fun you've allowed yourself to have in years.

The world hasn't become less interesting, less awe-inspiring;

our minds and egos have only started to cover our eyes with a veil.

You are a child of Mamma Earth's diversity.

You come from her and you walk within her changes, changing as you go.

You are reinvented every morning, so have no fear.

Flow with her, and dance with her moods

CHAPTER 9

DISCOVERING INNER ANCHORS

I long for peace,

But where on this wobbling, spinning globe is my sanctuary?

Sometimes, in my wandering mind, I dream that I once knew,

But where can I find one simple thought, one constant dream

To always guide me home?

For all my hopeful dewdrop thoughts of peace

Evaporate under this unsettled sun.

Where is the peace in this turbulent sea?

In this ocean of confusion, there is nothing to grasp,

nothing to anchor to, nothing to hold.

I searched all the maps of the globe, all the maps of the mind, until I found at last,

The peace is me,

I am

the sanctuary.

Thanks to human beings, this planet is not usually a very peaceful place most of the time. The peace that we do get does not last for long. People are rushing around all over, creating all kinds of noise and trouble as they go. Just being alive involves activity because we all need to move, to act, to do things, if we want to eat and to survive another day. It's hard to keep our balance.

Still, even amid all this bustling activity, there are moments of peace. We all taste it, occasionally.

In rare moments we can feel such bliss, such completion, such fulfillment, but then something mysterious happens. The peace fades, disappears, and leaves us feeling a little bit rushed and frustrated again.

There seems to be a troop of mischievous spirit monkeys at large and they rob us of peace all the time.

Sometimes we feel that we can know the truth of a peaceful life so deeply, and somehow, by some mysterious glitch of the mind, tomorrow we forget all about that truth. We're back where we started, worrying about our circumstances, fearing an outcome, dissatisfied with the results of yesterday.

Why does this happen?

It happens because we do not know ourselves fully, because we do not fully appreciate what we are, deep down, because we have no true, permanent inner anchor. We don't trust the self.

We are searching for peace out there.

Every movement toward the outside is a movement away from the center of peace.

We imagine that, if we find the right relationship and work hard at it, only then we will find inner peace and fulfillment. We imagine that, if we find the right job, a more peaceful job, one that pays better and with a better boss and pleasant co-workers, then we might finally be at peace. If only we won the lottery, then maybe we wouldn't have to worry. We could buy all the peace we need.

We might even imagine that if we finally create that meditation space, with all those nice candles and incense sticks, that perfect meditation playlist, and finally get down to meditating every day, and finally work up the energy to really, really try... then maybe, just maybe...

Something itches in the spirit, something drives us a little crazy, and we can't be at peace with who we are. Those crazy monkeys are rascals and they never leave us alone. Perhaps if other people would respect us more, we think, or love us more, or pay us more... maybe then we will find peace.

We may spend our entire lives trying to make other people happy, hoping that it will bring a sense of peace and completion into our own lives. Many of us spend a lot of time and energy trying to turn ourselves into the kinds of people that we imagine the world likes, just to measure up to some impossible benchmark.

The whole effort makes us inwardly tense and robs us of peace, for we can never succeed in a world where the goal keeps changing. What satisfies one person doesn't work for the next person, so we have no way to please everyone all the time.

We all want the security of a lasting kind of peace and a permanent inner joy that never changes, but we are searching for it in a place where *everything* is subject to the law of change. We cannot find permanent peace out there.

Our eyes are pointed in the wrong direction.

Only when we look within can we make peace with ourselves.

"But how do I make peace with myself," you ask, "because it's not as simple as it sounds? I've looked within, and trust me, it's a mess in here!"

To penetrate right into the core of the self, one has to dig through many layers of thoughts, beliefs, feelings, subconscious drives, fantasies, and dream stuff.

All the years of conditioning that we were subjected to while growing up, stand in the way of our true selves. The ideas we hold about who we are supposed to become, what we have to live up to—these beliefs veil our true nature. All the many personas and layers of veneer that we added to our essential being are obscuring the truth of who we are, deep inside.

None of those many, many onion layers contains anything permanent. Even the act of digging through all of this "mess" is still a movement away from peace.

Our thoughts are not permanent. They come and they go. So too, our beliefs can change. Our feelings arrive unexpectedly and we can't control them. We can't trust them to arise at the exact moment that we need them or to leave us alone when we don't want our feelings. These are still not the core of who we are. They are changing experiences, and we cannot get a grip on them.

Our deepest subconscious layers of mind usually only surface in our dreams, or during hypnosis, or in altered states of consciousness, and these deep layers are not permanent either. They too are subject to change, like turbulent waves on a stormy sea. They are not the source of our peace either.

These many layers around our central core of *being* contain all the things we desire and all the things we fear. They are the moving *content* of our life-stream, not the source. They are a little closer to the center than our outward circumstances of life, like our jobs and relationships, but they are still not essentially "me."

There is only one permanent, peaceful core, and it has no name.

It is not a thought, not a belief, not an intuition, not a feeling, and it is not an experience.

The core of self is the silent place from where we look at the world, from where we look at our thoughts, from where we observe our feelings, from where we see all our experiences, coming and going. The core, the essence of us, is the eye of the storm, around which our life rages in a spiral of movement.

Every attempt to change ourselves, every attempt to search, to seek, to manipulate, to improve something creates a kind of tension in us. We feel that tension behind our eyes, in our delicate neck muscles, in our spine, and in our gut.

Essentially, we are looking out from this infinitely peaceful place and we are looking with an attitude of judgment and criticism. Our motive may be to improve our state of peace, but we are looking outward with the question, "What's wrong here? What doesn't fit? What needs to change, so I can find peace?"

True self-knowing, true peace within the self, is to see that the very place from where we are looking, hoping, criticizing, trying to change things   the very source from where we are coming, is itself peaceful, and changeless.

When we recognize the peace that is already present here, we simply fall back into it, without trying to change a thing. That is how we make peace: We don't really make it, we allow ourselves to fall back into it and we stop trying to make anything at all.

There is no tension involved in that movement because it is a return home. It is not the energy of striving or reaching or clinging, but the energy of releasing, surrendering, and letting go. To look for peace outside of "me" is to close the hand in a fist. To find it inside me is to open my hand and relax the muscles.

Surrender to that which is already here and the peace reveals itself. It was always there but we forgot our home.

When we make this silent, infinite, graceful and living core our permanent home, then we find peace.

As we grow up and mature into adults, we begin to identify our sense of self with things *outside* of our essential self.

"I'm educated, sophisticated, well-read, and athletic," we tell ourselves, but these things are on the periphery of life. "I'm a mother, and a wife, and a hard worker," we may tell ourselves, but this means identifying our sense of self with attributes, with characteristics, with things that can change.

When we identify our sense of self with our core peace, then core peace becomes us. It permeates our cells, our brains, and it spontaneously moves outward into our lives, our relationships, our jobs, and every circumstance.

From this wellspring of peace, true self-knowledge arises and we can see the truth within any situation, within any circumstance. We are at home, always, no matter what role we need to play in life today.

From this center point, the truth is self-evident. The only person that can truly upset me is me.

I have the power to hurt myself and I have the power to benefit myself. To blame others, to blame circumstances, to blame genetics or anything else is to create self-division and rob me of my real power.

If I do not choose to be happy, nobody else can make me happy. If I choose to be happy, nobody else can make me unhappy. To understand this is to know myself and to make peace with myself.

I make my life what it is. I decide what my life means. I am the one who creates my joy and I am the one who creates and sustains my suffering and depression.

There are things outside of me that can bring me temporary joy or cause me temporary pain, but it is my own choice to identify with those things, to give them power over me, and to believe the story in my head that I create about those things.

This kind of self-realization is the golden key to finding inner stillness, the key to overcoming negative self-speech, and the key to inner peace.

Find the essence of life within and make it your anchor, your sanctuary. It is so mysterious, so simple, so intuitive. Explore this inspirational, cosmic, tranquil space. Get to know it intimately, in-depth, and you will find nothing but peace.

Willpower, brute force, and self-criticism will stand in the way of finding peace. How would you make peace with a loved one? Would you *fight* for peace? Would you highlight all their faults and explain in detail why you are right and they are wrong? Or would you approach them humbly, with love, reassuringly, and kindly?

Do you not deserve the same thoughtfulness when making peace with yourself? Be the loved one that you are.

Embrace the totality of what you are, and that includes embracing your wild, natural side, along with your faults, your talents, and all your quirks. Those are your attributes, not your essential self.

A great illustration here is to observe the way that a trickle of water finds its way to the river. As the water moves, it looks as if it is putting out fingers into the landscape, feeling its way. One finger of the little stream of water runs into a dead end. There is a stone or some high ground, and it just stops there. The water doesn't neurotically try to force its way through. It doesn't judge itself as having failed. It simply finds its way around and continues, using nothing but the force of gravity to find the best, most efficient way to where it is going.

Only human beings take dead ends to be judgments on our worth. Only we try to force our way through things that don't want to be forced. Only we make such foolish mistakes when life is actually guiding us all the time. Every "dead end" is just a message: "Hey, this way is difficult, why not find another way around?"

Find your state of flow. When your ego is out of the way and you act from a spontaneous choiceless place, just like water, then your desires are the same as the universe's desires. Then flow happens. Great creativity happens in a creative, exquisite dance and it doesn't feel like hard work.

You are the architect of your own life, the master of your destiny. Within your grasp lies the power to define the very meaning of your existence. Understand that the joy and the suffering, the elation and the despair, all reside within the realm of your choices. External circumstances may offer temporary solace or anguish, but it is your conscious decision to identify with them, to grant them authority over your being, and to craft the stories in your mind that shape your reality.

In this profound self-realization, you unlock the golden key to inner stillness, a sanctuary of tranquility that transcends negative self-talk. Look deep within and discover the essence of life that resides in the depths of your soul, an intuitive and cosmic force that yearns for connection. Immerse yourself in this boundless wellspring of inspiration, where peace becomes your faithful companion.

Let go of the notion that willpower, brute force, and self-criticism will pave the path to serenity. Reflect on how you would make peace with a loved one. Would you engage in battle, highlighting their faults and defending your righteousness? Or would you approach them with humility, love, and gentle reassurance? Extend the same thoughtfulness and compassion to yourself, for you too are deserving of healing.

Embrace the totality of who you are—the wild, untamed facets, the flaws, the talents, and the idiosyncrasies. They are the colorful brushstrokes that compose your unique canvas. But remember, they do not define your essential self. Find your state of flow, where the ego dissipates, and you act from a place of choiceless spontaneity. In this harmonious dance, your desires align with the universe's desires and great creativity unfolds with exquisite beauty.

You hold within you the capacity for profound self-love and acceptance. Embrace the boundless potential that flows through your veins and let it guide you to a place of unwavering tranquility. Trust in your innate wisdom, and honor the divine essence that resides within. For in this journey of self-discovery, you will find not only peace but a profound connection to the limitless universe that surrounds you. You are... an embodiment of love, grace, and infinite possibilities.

CHAPTER 10

CHOOSING JOY: FROM THE PINNACLE TO THE RIVER'S EDGE

You may well find the feeling of success on the pinnacle of the mountain,

But the joy of life that you seek from success is not there.

That high peak is barren and cold.

Your true pleasure grows thickest near the river at the bottom of the valley,

and the joy thins out more, the higher you climb.

It can easily happen in life that we become stuck in a rut. We can wear out the same comfortable pathways, day after day. We can repeat our habits mechanically and we feel as if we are going nowhere.

In such a condition of soul, there is little joy of life, for there is nothing new and there is no richness, no texture, and no deep, intriguing subtext to our existence. All we are doing is going through the motions, waiting for our lives to begin or waiting for our lives to be over.

"How can I motivate myself?" We might ask ourselves.

There are two completely different approaches.

The first kind of motivation springs from a great soul abundance. It's the sort of motivation that we're really after. This approach arises naturally from an overflowing fountainhead of inner energy and creativity.

It's when we have so much to give, so much buzzing inside, that we simply have to share it, express it, and spread the feeling. It spills over from within. It feels effortless and wholesome all on its own. Filled with unexplainable joy, we wake up energized, curious to see what the day will bring, ready for anything. Ideas just arrive, and we somehow know exactly what to do with those ideas.

We might call this approach a heart-centered motivation.

There is another kind of motivation that is very different. This method is based on willpower and rigid control. Instead of an overflow, it springs from a lack of energy and we have to fight that sense of lack, that sense of dullness, that sense of lethargy with fear. We have to goad ourselves with a stick and we have to lure ourselves with a carrot.

We constantly hold up the fear of losing ground, of slipping backward, of failing. We have to force it to move forward. We have to bribe ourselves with visions of what our efforts will bring us.

We tell ourselves (or someone threatens us) that we're going to miss out, we're going to fail if we don't bring our best game. With this approach, we have the habit of postponing our satisfaction in life until the goal is reached.

We might call this head-centered or ego-centered motivation.

It's a curious thing. Sometimes the worst thing we can do is to achieve our dream. Now, that may sound counter-intuitive, especially in a chapter dedicated to the theme of motivation, but the point is that, without our big dream, the rest of our lives can seem empty. Did you know that there is a form of mental imbalance called post-achievement depression?

It happens more often than you might think. World champion athletes, Olympians, business people at the top of their game, great academics and scientists, and people from many different walks of life have experienced it to different degrees. They achieve the pinnacle of their careers; they reach the highest peak—and then comes the question, "What now?"

Our brain chemistry produces dopamine, which has been called the "achievement hormone." The dopamine hit that the brain produces with success is addictive but, now that the peak is achieved, there is no way to access another hit. It's similar, in some ways, to the experience of a drug user who tries to give up the addiction. Highly driven people will sometimes encounter this feeling and it can lead to a breakdown.

Suddenly the other dimensions of their lives resolve into perspective and the picture isn't pretty. They have sacrificed everything to achieve that big goal, but once the initial feeling of success and glory wears off, there's nothing solid underneath.

Discarded relationships lie strewn on the pathway, broken and irretrievable. Countless hours of effort and sacrifice now seem worth far less than they did at the beginning of the journey. Suddenly their priorities come into question. Was it true *motivation*, or some kind of compulsive *fear* of not being enough? Their self-worth was so identified, so tangled up with achieving that goal, and now it all seems to crumble.

The truth of it all hits home like a sucker punch: The old cliché contained more wisdom than they suspected. The real joy is in the journey, not the destination.

The rest of us are puzzled. You have it all, so how can you be unhappy?

You see, we have forgotten an important detail. What an authentic, living human being is looking for is not the temporary feeling of elation that comes from some achievement, but *permanent* peace and joy. We want a feeling of fulfillment that lasts. We want a long-term motivation that sustains us.

We tend to forget that all personal growth happens while we are going through it. We think it's a problem but it is what engages us. All the fun is in that quest. Our single-minded exclusion of everything but our end goal robs us of the choicest morsels that life has to offer. We can't go back and start again because the motivation is no longer there. What now?

So it raises the question: Is there any point in motivating ourselves in the first place? It's a good question, and one worth asking. It deserves a balanced answer.

When we wholeheartedly engage our living, vital energy with the present,

then we experience a feedback loop.

It's a state of flow.

CHAPTER 11

BEYOND ACHIEVEMENT: THE JOY OF BEING

We live in an achiever's culture, especially in the Western world. If we don't "make it," then we are made to feel like underachievers, at least compared to all those bright stars on the covers of those magazines, all those faces on the television, and all those profile pages on social media.

From a young age, we are motivated to live up to our potential, to strive, to seek, and to reach for our dream. We label people as winners or losers. Not all of us take the bait, but most of us do.

We dream of what may be. After all, if we never reach for the stars, how can we possibly reach the sky? Without the proper motivation, wouldn't we just degenerate into couch potatoes?

There's nothing worse than a wasted life—or so we are told, and we can all sense a grain of truth in this kind of thinking.

"What would you like to be when you grow up?" If you're anything like me, then you heard that one a hundred times as a kid.

Which one of us is born with the wisdom to answer, "It doesn't matter all that much. I know it will be great. That which I already am is enough and what I *do* with that is secondary."

Our parents would have thought we were weird if we had answered in that way. People take life very seriously, so in all likelihood, we would not have gotten a good response.

Subtly, our happiness is equated with our success. What we *do* is mistaken for *who we are*.

"What do you *do* for a living?" People ask this question first and it tells them everything they want to know about us. They are more interested in the exterior than the interior.

As children, people don't ask us, "What are you going to do with your time and energy when you grow up?" They ask us, "What are you going to *be*?" It implies that in some important way, we don't exist yet. We are still unfinished, still a work in progress, and it implies that we can only be whole when we *become* something.

Buying this misunderstanding, swallowing it hook, line, and sinker, we invest our emotional energy, and our sense of self-worth into the story of our success. It means, in the language of psychology, that we invest a locus of control into an exterior source or, in simpler language, we give our power away.

We reschedule the full joy of living until the moment we achieve the goal. "When I get there, I will be complete, whole, and happy. Until then, it's a struggle, so there's no time for savoring life."

That goal could be anything: Buying a house, falling in love, having children, earning a good salary, getting a degree, or reaching the pinnacle of achievement.

As a result, we find ourselves postponing our joy of life indefinitely. We have touched on this theme already, but it bears repeating here: From the time that we are children, our life is presented to us as a series of hurdles to jump, a series of milestones that we have to reach, so we can measure up. We think of our lives as a linear thing—from point A to point B, then on to point C and beyond.

We have to make it to first grade and, as soon as we do, the goalpost shifts. Now we have to make it to second grade. We have to finally graduate from school, only to find that another goal post has materialized. We may have to go through college or get that degree. Half of the people that attain their Ph.D. will suffer from some form of post-achievement depression, but that's not the end of it.

Then we enter the rat race and, mysteriously, new goalposts keep appearing. We have to pay those bills and invest in our future. That unending ladder needs to be climbed. We have to struggle to make enough money to retire comfortably—maybe *then* we will be able to relax and smell the roses.

We never really get the sensation of having arrived at the final destination. Satisfaction is postponed indefinitely. We have sold our life energy to an idea and now we feel like beggars, not emperors in our inner kingdom.

Our eyes are looking ahead to the future and we are missing the present moment. We have invested our total sense of identity, along with all our heart, into a single goal—into the future. We forget about the present moment or take it for granted, treating it like a stepping-stone.

But our lives are not linear. There are dimensions in life that cannot be put in a straight line, for they have depth and a vibrant quality that defies time. The energy of the heart does not move from point A to point B; it cannot be measured and quantified—it can only be lived, only experienced.

Imagine for a moment that you have achieved all your big goals. You've made all the money, you've got the dream lifestyle, you have created amazing work, you have gained the love and respect of all those people.

Will the present moment feel any different? Will your core essence change in any significant way? Will your quality of heart be any different? Or will you still feel the same inside your skin?

People who have reached that point will admit that it feels a little uncomfortable and there's a nagging kind of question in their gut: "Is this all there is?" Often, a moment of great success is a moment of great disillusionment.

They begin to realize that their self-worth is dependent on *doing*, on achieving, on winning, and not on simply being. People admire them for their achievements, for their bank balance, for their nice home, but not *for who they really are*. It's as if all the accolades belong to a fake.

Of course, not every successful person is the same, but so often, underneath the great success story, underneath the clothing of achievement, they often feel naked and unfulfilled. They may not be able to admit the sense that there is something incomplete in them.

Their drive came from an inability to rest in their essential nature, from the ceaseless movement away from their perceived "small self," their "unworthy self," toward a grandiose vision. The ego was in control, and it got them to the top of the mountain in one way or another, but it simultaneously cheated them out of an authentic feeling of joy.

They have missed the truth of living, chasing the imaginary, forgetting what is real.

Those "success stories" where people honestly feel fulfilled are different. They are satisfied by a feeling deep inside, deep in their hearts, and the outward success is only a mirror of their inner state.

What does "success" look and feel like to you? Is it defined by material things? Or, is it an internal state?

When we are not present when we live in ideas only,

then we sell the energy of our existence cheaply.

CHAPTER 12

THE ART OF STILLNESS: FINDING SERENITY IN THE PRESENT

In the realm of the present,

where the threads of life intricately entwine,

we find ourselves.

Here, there is no need to dwell in the burdens of tomorrow,

or the weight of the past.

We are invited to embrace the essence of now,

where existence unfolds with profound significance.

Here we find our serenity, here we find our peace.

The present moment is *the time of your life*. It's all happening *now*. This is it and you are it. You are living it, right now, and it is happening for you, in this moment; not tomorrow, not yesterday, but now.

It's one thing to understand this intellectually, but quite another thing to truly embody this insight. When this deep sense of presence, of aliveness, becomes part of the heart, when it becomes part of the cellular expression of life, part of the bones and sinews, reflected in body language, voice tone, and facial expression—then this insight *lives* in us. Then there is no need for external motivation, for inside all is movement, all is dance.

Our ego-minds worry about tomorrow but nothing ever happens tomorrow, for when "tomorrow" arrives, it appears as the present moment.

When the present moment is filled with the desire to be somewhere else, the fear of not being in the right place at the right time, the fear of not being, or having enough, then life loses its energy and we feel depleted.

When we are not present, when we live in ideas only, then we sell the energy of our existence cheaply. We sell it to an idea, to a concept of happiness, investing in a specter of fear, instead of the real, joyous thing. We disregard the living reality right here with us, treating it as a means to an end

We cannot reach a tomorrow that is full of hope and energy from this place, because we drag that feeling of not being enough with us into "tomorrow," which is just another iteration of *now*.

This is why so many of us feel a lack of motivation as if we are stuck in life.

Our living *energy* is stuck and unavailable for dynamic interaction with life. Most of the energy is invested in the future, which may or may not happen. There is not enough energy left over for engaging with what is happening right now.

What we thought was motivating us is leeching our energy. Our heart intelligence knows this or at least suspects it. This is why we feel that there is a war between the heart and the mind. We know what we should be doing, what we want to be doing, but somehow we're doing the opposite.

We can't accumulate an abundance of élan vital, of chi, of mojo when we invest all our power in fantasy. When we hold back, waiting for the right time, the energy slowly leaks out. To get the kind of experience we want out of life, we have to give our energy generously, totally, and freely to what is between our hands, right here, right where our feet are planted on the ground.

When we wholeheartedly engage our living, vital energy with the present, we experience a feedback loop. It's a state of flow.

Our energy bounces back from *whatever* we are doing and rewards us with the feeling of living—of really living. The vibrating reality outside our skin mirrors our inner state of feeling real.

We feel—yes! *This* is it. This is happening, and this is where all the action, all the adventure is. We feel engaged, flowing, and switched on. Hours may pass and they seem like just minutes. We feel motivated, but now the motivation is effortless. It does not depend on outer circumstances. It no longer depends on the approval of others. Success and failure do not enter our thoughts. We don't feel like winners and we don't feel like losers; instead, we simply feel like our authentic selves.

The stick-and-carrot approach may work for a while, but never permanently. That approach to motivation tends to divide us on the inside. The head says one thing: "I have to exercise more, I have to study, I have to improve myself" but the heart says something else: "It doesn't satisfy me. Why bother?"

We can reconcile these two parts of our inner world. The head and the heart can speak to each other in a friendly way. They can become dance partners instead of archenemies.

The way to do that is by becoming aware of a deeper substratum of life and by resting in our sense of being, knowing that it is enough. It is so much more than enough!

Just appreciating life and the simplest things can refill our wellsprings of energy so that they once again begin to overflow. Stop wasting precious life energy on things that do not serve you. Stop wasting power on feeling anxious, on feeling unworthy, on feeling guilty, and the energy begins to accumulate.

When our energy is no longer constantly leaking out, trying to fulfill some kind of impossible list of expectations, then it naturally gathers in our system.

We have storehouses of energy within us and one of the biggest is located near our belly button. (It's identified by different names in different schools, including the hara, the dantien, the Cinnabar field, the elixir, and other names. It is where we experience that "gut feeling." If you place your hands on this area and quietly explore your inner sensations there, you can get an intuitive sense of this energy storehouse, right in the middle of you.)

Love yourself enough to fill your inner warehouse of love. Fill the tanks and then there is plenty to share.

When enough energy accumulates inside us, it begins to overflow. It wants to burst out of us in laughter, activity, creativity, compassion, and through helping the world around us. We feel inspired. We feel healthy and vital.

We feel like going for walks. We feel that we want to dance or just tell someone how much we admire and appreciate them. We want to cook wonderful meals and enjoy eating those meals, and go outside and look at the stars, or dance in the soft rain. Why? Simply for the joy of being. Simply because we are in the present moment, and we are soaking in the experience. We are enjoying life, instead of thinking about it, planning for it, or trying to explain it away.

There's no goal, there's no destination—we simply want to act. It's natural and spontaneous, it is choiceless and the rewards of our actions are merely the cherry on top. We move because of the joy of movement; we create for the love of creating.

Joy levitates us. Joy lifts us. Joy is the antidote to the gravity of depression and self-division. Joy is a motivation unto itself.

This is a heart-centered motivation and it doesn't fade, leaving us feeling cheated or lost. It can become the background feeling to life, sustaining us in all that we undertake.

It doesn't always provide the same high that achieving a major life goal provides, but it doesn't let us crash in a heap afterward.

Like water, it is gentle, soft, and nourishing. It sustains our life. It flows on and we can flow with it.

This heart motivation is not the enemy of the mind. It can use practical, rational mental strategies to take care of practical problems, to prepare for the winter, to make our way through the traffic, to budget, and to plan, but it does not become trapped by those activities. It moves from a place of abundant caring, not lack, not need, not compulsion.

Like water, it flows around all obstacles, carving its way gracefully through the environment, nurturing all living things along the way without discrimination or judgment.

Our thoughts are not our enemies. Our egos are not our enemies, but they make terrible slave masters.

There's nothing wrong with thinking or with trains of thought, or thought processes. Wishful thinking can be fun sometimes. It can be enjoyable to imagine all the things we would do if we had a million dollars. The danger comes when we mistake our thoughts, our dreams, and our wishes for our lived reality. Our wishes become poisonous, in a subtle way, when we start believing that we can be happy only if the wish comes true.

The thoughts in our heads are powerless until we ignite them, and supercharge them with life spirit. Emotions are driving energy. When we holistically and wisely link our thoughts and emotions together with the body, then life is encountered fully, and wholeheartedly.

How do we create joy? We don't have to. It's already there, underneath everything else. All we have to do is become quiet inside and rediscover what's already there—always available.

Shift your state of feeling, shift your way of thinking, and your life changes. It's not that life has to change first, and then we feel good emotions or think good thoughts. It's the other way around. First, we change our state, then the experience of life around us conforms and mirrors our inner state. Fall back into your real, authentic self, and motivation follows in your wake.

We need to focus on lifting our spirits to soaring heights beyond the constraints of everyday existence. Joyful love is a force that defies gravity, propelling us into a realm where possibilities are infinite and dreams take flight. In the presence of true joy, our souls alight with a radiant glow and our hearts beat in sync with the rhythm of the universe. Our actions rhyme with the cosmos.

It is in those moments of pure elation that we get a glimpse of life's greatest wonders. The mundane is transformed into the extraordinary and the ordinary becomes extraordinary. Every breath becomes a celebration, every step an exquisite dance. Joy whispers in the wind, painting rainbows across the sky and weaving magic into the fabric of our existence.

When joy finds its dwelling place within us, it ignites a spark that sets our passions ablaze. It fuels our creativity, illuminates our path, and fuels our pursuit of the extraordinary. We become catalysts of love and inspiration, radiating warmth and compassion to all who cross our paths. Joy becomes our compass, guiding us toward a life filled with purpose, meaning, and deep fulfillment.

So, my dear friend, embrace joy as if it were a divine gift bestowed upon you. Allow it to permeate every fiber of your being, to infuse your days with its enchanting fragrance. Let joy be the wings that carry you through life's challenges and the anchor that grounds you in gratitude and contentment. For in the realm of joy, you will discover a wellspring of resilience, hope, and unwavering faith in the beauty of this incredible journey we call life.

Embrace joy, and watch as it levitates you to heights beyond imagination. Embrace joy, and let its transformative power touch every aspect of your existence. You are a vessel of joy, a beacon of light in a world yearning for its radiance. So, spread your wings, my dear friend, and let the joy within you soar, for it is in your embrace of joy that you truly come alive.

Joy levitates us.

It is in those moments of pure elation that we get a glimpse of life's greatest wonders.

The mundane is transformed into the extraordinary, and the ordinary becomes extraordinary.

Every breath becomes a celebration, every step an exquisite dance.

Joy whispers in the wind, painting rainbows across the sky and weaving magic into the fabric of our existence.

CHAPTER 13

DISCOVERING YOUR INTRINSIC PURPOSE

Where stars twinkle in cosmic ballet,

a journey lies,

To reveal life's intrinsic purpose.

With wings unfurled, like a fragile butterfly,

we step onto the shimmering path,

woven with golden threads.

Guided by the wind's whispered secrets,

through verdant valleys and majestic peaks,

we traverse boundless landscapes,

illuminated by the sun's gentle caress.

Within this symphony of existence,

our souls ignite with a fiery spark,

and as purpose unfolds.

The thing that you are looking for, to motivate you, to give your life meaning, to give you direction—is you.

The goal you are chasing, to feel whole and happy—is you. The love you are longing for, the feeling of belonging in this cosmos, of being cherished, adored, of being in the right place at the right time—is you.

Your purpose, in other words—is *you*.

Our hearts can understand this idea intuitively, but our minds get in the way. We may feel that it's nice to say these uplifting, poetic kinds of things and maybe stick them on the fridge door, but really, they have no meaning. They don't make *sense* practically. They don't answer some important philosophical, spiritual, and psychological questions. It's not a rational answer, so how do we *use* that information?

Let's look at this idea a little more closely and try to dig into what we mean when we say that *you are* your very own purpose.

How does that help? In fact, it is the most wonderfully practical thing to understand. It can free us up inwardly in a tremendously meaningful way if we get the essence of it.

The word "purpose" is all about utility and usefulness. Purpose means the underlying reasons, intentions, and determination, and it depends on cause and effect.

We might say, "Wow, that woman seems so confident. She walks with purpose and poise and seems so perfectly put together."

A little brother who is the victim of a practical joke might accuse his older sister, "You did that on purpose!"

For instance, we might ask, "What is the *purpose* of this meeting?" (And we might get annoyed if the meeting goes on and on, and accomplishes nothing). Are you nodding your head? You know the feeling!

You see, the idea of purpose implies that strange little question, "Why?" Why did you do it? Why did this happen? Why did you create that? Why is it here? Why go on in this way? (I have been quite famous in my life for asking everyone and myself these questions since I was a child and maybe you are a "why" person too!)

It implies that somebody knows what they want, and they made a plan to get it—on purpose.

Moreover, the trouble with that little question ("Why?") is that it never really has a satisfying answer, because you can always ask it one more time. Children will often go through a phase in their early development when they constantly ask, "Why?" It can be exasperating. A conversation that typically happens with my little ones often sounds like this:

"Mommy, *why* do you have to go?"

"Because I have to work."

"But *why*?"

"Because if I don't work, I don't earn any money, and then we can't have this nice home, or food to eat—you see?"

"But *why*?

"Well, that's just the way the world works. Things cost money."

There's a little pause to digest that, but then comes another one.

"Why?"

"Well, I don't know. It's always been this way."

"But why..."

And no matter how beautifully you answer the question, a curious child can always dig a little deeper, and keep asking another "Why?" until we get right down to the bedrock of nature and question existence itself. Why anything at all? Most of us give up long before it gets to that point.

At some point, we give up trying to provide information and we have to admit, "I don't really know." If we have enough patience, we can guide a curious child's mind by asking questions in return, but if we're at our wit's end, we may simply dismiss the child, and say angrily, "Just because!"

Deep underneath our ideas about purpose, and specifically, our ideas about our sense of purpose, is this same annoying question: Why anything at all?

Our questions are tools for our rational minds so that we can probe the world around us and figure out how things fit together. Questions are wonderful in that sense. They are light-seeking tools.

There's a glitch, though. Questions always breed more questions. We can go on studying everything in the universe for an entire lifetime and we will end up with more questions than we had when we started. Our egos become inflated with all our head knowledge but our egos are never totally satisfied. There's always at least one more question that needs an answer.

Anyone seriously interested in discovering the purpose of their life will find an incredible amount of information out there, books upon books, teachers upon teachers, and podcasts aplenty, but very few simple, intuitive answers.

We can pursue a philosophical inquiry or a spiritual one. We can look for it in psychology, in literature, in science, and there are many more routes besides these. Eventually, we end up with more questions than answers.

This is because we are looking in the wrong place again and using the wrong tool for the job.

The rational mind is always going to be plagued by doubt. Its job is to doubt everything so that it can penetrate more deeply into matters. It keeps analyzing, it keeps asking questions. That's why there is no end to science, no ultimate answer to the big "why?"

Because it is such a powerful tool and because it seems to be the only faculty that we have by which we can make sense of things, the ego mind assumes the throne of self. We begin to believe that we *are* our minds, that we *are* the questions and answers that circle in our heads. We are forever incomplete because there is always one more "why?"

We cannot find a satisfying answer to the ultimate existential question—"why"—using only the tool of rational discrimination. We need something more powerful, something more intuitive.

For an answer to the question, "What is my purpose?" to have genuine power in our lives, it has to ring true in our hearts. Theory alone is not enough.

There's another problem. The rational mind cannot be truly spontaneous. It studies information and traces links between ideas. The mind collects facts and organizes those facts into pleasing patterns of meaning. But ask a rational mind: *Why* do I feel like dancing? *Why* did I fall in love? *Why* was my grandmother so dear to me? *Why* do I like the taste of homemade soup and cinnamon buns so much? And the rational mind struggles.

Sure enough, it can attempt to explain anything at all in a rational way, but the answers are not satisfying; at least, not deeply. We get the impression that the mind is posturing. It's just making stuff up.

When we consider the natural world around us, it seems to be doing some incredible things without one needing to think rationally about anything at all. It doesn't worry about purpose. It doesn't worry about "why." Nature is its own "why."

There are so many stars in the universe that it numbs our minds. Why is the universe so big and so complicated? Living things are such miraculously complicated arrangements of atoms that modern science has hardly scratched the surface of their nature. From the "simplest" proteins and amino acids right up to the cosmic complexity of the human brain, nature has a stupendously complex and spontaneous intelligence that has inspired our science for hundreds of years. It will go on inviting us to discover for many centuries to come.

How does your pituitary gland know what to do? How do you grow hair and fingernails? How do you heal your skin when it is cut or bruised? Does your clever rational mind have to provide instructions? Does it need to know *why*? How do ecosystems know how to maintain equilibrium and what accounts for the marvelous variety of life forms on this planet? Why is it here, doing its incredible dance?

When we look at nature, we find a spontaneous, universal kind of harmony. We can call it intelligence, or design, or self-patterning, but those are just words and theories. It is what it is—and it is astounding!

We human beings come out of this majestic existence. We are self-patterning, self-guided, and spontaneously arising wonders of complexity. We are so intricate that we can form words, ideas, and images in our minds, and communicate those ideas in all kinds of ways with other human beings.

Then, pasted on top of all this mystery and complexity like a plastic veneer, we have this little question: "Why?" We forget to put that question into the proper context.

When we use our heart intelligence to approach this question of purpose, the question melts.

Our hearts know the answer. The universe is all connected, and we are woven into its fabric with all other beings, all other things in the cosmos. It is what it is and it is exploring what it wants to become next.

We are answers to the universe's ongoing question: What would it be like to become...? (fill in the blank).

And we can provide any answer we choose.

We are forever becoming what we are, one moment at a time. We are forever exploring the depths and intricacies of being human, of love, of relationships, of food, of dance and poetry, of science and numbers, of spirituality, of boredom, of sickness and trouble, and how to overcome those many, many challenges.

Some of us feel like we were born to be something. It might be a healer, a teacher, an inventor, or something else. Or we feel we were meant for more, somehow. Some of us just do not feel that way and that's okay too.

It can be terribly confusing and it can make us question our self-worth. All our friends and peers seem to be choosing careers, choosing lines of study, and heading for a goal but here we are, wondering what we're supposed to do. Lost.

We don't feel we're meant for any one specific role in this life but, rather, we are exploring lots of different dimensions simultaneously. You would be surprised how many people feel this way.

Even while the question of our ultimate purpose in life seems to be on hold, we are exploring what it means to be children or parents. We are playing with how to succeed or fail in those roles. We are exploring what it means to be wealthy or what it means to struggle financially. We want the feeling of beating the odds and making our way through guts, determination, and perseverance. Some of us are exploring music. Others are exploring nature. Some of us are searching everywhere for something that lights us up.

Does it matter? We are following our love.

This universe is a game, but a game of such miraculous richness that we have to gasp in awe, call it "Holy!" and simply enjoy the unexplainable wonder of just being here, just being alive, taking part in all of this. From this inner space of gratitude, awe, and humility, we sense that it is all happening for us, at least, right now. Tomorrow it will be the turn of another being.

Within this game, we can come up with any purpose that we like. We can explain things in any way that makes sense to us, based on where we are in our journey. We can find endless reasons for things if we want to—because it is fascinating, after all—or we can simply live, and *be* that purpose, *be* that reason, *be* that explanation.

The canvas of your purpose lies wide open, awaiting the brushstrokes of your intentions. You hold the power to shape and define the very essence of your existence. You can craft any purpose that resonates with the depths of your soul, aligning with your values, passions, and aspirations. In this boundless realm, you have the freedom to create meaning and significance that reflects your journey.

The beauty of it all is that there are no limitations, no fixed rules, or predetermined paths. You have the freedom to explore, to wander, to seek, and create. You are the architect of your purpose, and the world becomes your playground of possibilities. It is in this wondrous dance between self-discovery and self-creation that the true essence of your being unfolds.

In my mind, this is why the whole thing exists in the first place!

You may choose to delve into the mysteries of existence, finding endless reasons and explanations that fuel your curiosity and wonder. Or perhaps you want to find solace in simply being, allowing the magnificence of your existence to be the very purpose that guides you. Each breath, each step, each heartbeat becomes an affirmation of your worthiness and your right to embrace the fullness of life.

So, my dear friend, embrace the power within you to choose your purpose. Let your heart be your compass and listen closely to the whispers of your soul. Trust in the wisdom that resides deep within you, for it knows the path that will lead you to fulfillment and joy. Embrace the journey of self-discovery, for it is within that exploration that your purpose will reveal itself, like a hidden gem waiting to be unearthed.

Remember, you are the author of your own story. Your purpose is a reflection of your inner truth, a guiding light that illuminates the path toward a life that is aligned with your deepest desires and values. Embrace this profound gift of choice and let your purpose be a testament to your unique essence, your boundless potential, and your unwavering capacity to love and be loved.

So step forward with courage, curiosity, and an open heart. Embrace the grand adventure of discovering and embracing your purpose, for in doing so, you will unleash the extraordinary power that resides within you. The world awaits your unique contribution and, as you embrace your purpose, you will inspire others to do the same. Embrace the beauty of choice, for it is in choosing your purpose that you will truly come alive.

CHAPTER 14

EMBODIED LOVE: BEYOND THEORY, INTO BEING

Love is not an intellectual thing. Real love instantly loses its vibrant authenticity when it becomes theoretical. When we turn love into an object, into something that we can study and analyze in a lab; when we think of it as something "out there," which is separate from me, the observer of love, then love becomes abstract. It becomes meaningless.

We can say all kinds of things about love. We can speak endlessly about true love and unconditional love. We can write books, invent theories, compose poems or write songs about it; but to really, really know what it is, we have to *live* it. We have to *become* it. Love has to dance a cosmic dance within us, through us, and by means of us.

Without this direct, existential, full-body-mind experience of love, we remain ignorant about its power and its wisdom. We cannot suspect its subtleties; we cannot know its fragrance and its perfume. When love is merely an idea in the mind, then it has no joy, no electricity, no power to move.

Is this not the main reason why it is so difficult to love oneself?

It's a nice idea—but how on earth?

We might turn it into our goal: "At some point in the future, I am going to prioritize and focus on self-love..."

Unfortunately, we cannot think our way to that goal. Projected into the future, our love remains out of reach. We will never achieve it by force and we cannot manipulate anyone to reach our goal, least of all ourselves. We can't fool ourselves here because, if we try to trick ourselves into loving ourselves, we will know. There is no way to plan, design, and engineer self-love.

We have to *become* that love. We have to embody it, fully and spontaneously. Only then does it flow from the self, into the self, through the self. Only then does it truly bless those around us.

One of the biggest reasons that we cannot find self-love is because we misunderstand its source. In other words, we do not directly know what the *self is*. We may have read about it. We may have heard people speak about it, we may have thought about it, however deeply, but it remains just an idea.

The self is so immediate, so close to us, so ever-present that it is completely invisible.

It's like trying to see your eyeballs or trying to find your head by looking for it out there. It's like a constant background hum, a noise that is going on all time, and we forget completely that it is there until the noise stops. It's like that picture on the wall at home. We have looked at that image so often that it has almost become invisible, almost a part of us. It's only when a friend notices the picture and points out a little detail, that we look at the picture again. "Oh yes, that old thing. I completely forgot about it."

It is like that with the self. It is always with us. It is always in us, living *as* us—it's where we are coming from—it's so utterly obvious, so direct, that we miss it completely. We speak about the "self," but all of our talk is theory, not real. The reality of self-knowing comes before our language.

When what we call ourselves is an idea, when it is just a word, only a concept, just a repetition of something we have heard, then our grasp of its essence is based on a misunderstanding. We can't know ourselves second-hand, we can only know this thing intimately—if we know it first-hand.

Love is a profound and visceral experience that transcends intellectual understanding. It is not a concept to be dissected in laboratories or confined within the boundaries of theories and analysis. Love loses its essence when it becomes detached from our lived experiences and turns into an abstract notion. It is in the living, the becoming, that love truly thrives.

We can discuss love endlessly, weave intricate tales of true and unconditional love, and express it through various art forms, but the depth of love can only be truly known through immersion. Love is meant to dance within us, flowing through every fiber of our being. It moves within us, by means of us, and for us.

Without this direct and immersive experience of love, we remain ignorant of its power and wisdom. We cannot fathom its subtleties or savor its fragrance. Love, when confined to the mind, loses its joy, its electric energy, and its ability to move us.

Perhaps this is why loving oneself is often a daunting task. We may appreciate the idea but struggle to embrace it fully. We make plans to prioritize self-love in the future, but such goals remain distant and unattainable as long as they are confined to the realm of thought. Love cannot be forced, manipulated, or tricked, especially not by ourselves.

To truly love oneself, we must embody love. We must allow it to flow from within us, naturally and spontaneously. It is through this embodiment that love blesses not only ourselves but also those around us.

One of the reasons self-love eludes us is because we misunderstand its source. We lack direct knowledge of the self. We may have encountered descriptions, conversations, and reflections about the self, but it often remains an intangible concept. The self is so intimately close to us, so ever-present, that it becomes invisible. It is like trying to see our eyeballs or find our head by searching for it externally.

The self is like a familiar picture hanging on our wall. We have grown accustomed to its presence, so much so that we overlook it completely until someone else points out its beauty. Similarly, the self is constantly with us, living as us, and yet we often overlook its existence. We talk about the self, but our words remain theoretical until we directly experience self-knowing.

When the self is reduced to a mere idea, a word, or a concept borrowed from others, our understanding of its essence becomes flawed. We cannot truly know ourselves through second-hand information; we can only intimately know this thing called the self through firsthand experience.

Let us embark on a profound exploration of the self. Let us dive deep and encounter it directly, free from preconceived notions and borrowed knowledge. In doing so, we will gain a clearer understanding of how the self intertwines with the concept of self-love.

May this journey bring us closer to the core of our being, where love resides, waiting to be recognized, embraced, and celebrated.

As an experiment, let's embark on a deeper exploration of this thing we call the "self." Let's get to know it directly, so we can more clearly see how it relates to what we are calling "self-love."

CHAPTER 15

UNVEILING THE ESSENCE OF EXISTENCE

In the ethereal essence,

where time dances like dewdrops,

existence's heartbeat thrives.

A delicate breeze whispers,

through ancient trees it drifts,

carrying stars' symphony and universe's secrets.

Rhythm of existence pulses,

through atoms, every breath,

the moon's glow upon rolling waves.

Boundless expanse reveals,

fleeting sparks, intertwined souls,

echoing creation's timeless melodies.

Instead of speaking about religions, metaphysics, or philosophics, let's look at this important question in a child-like way, simply, and let's look at it directly.

Each one of us can say, "I am." We can say it in all honesty, without explaining it, without needing to justify it in any way at all. This is the first, most primal truth that there is—not so? But let me ask you this: What is it like to *be*?

The question is not about your life story, your experiences, your likes, and dislikes, or your attributes—not the *content* of your life, not at all. What we want to know is: What is it like *to exist*?

What can you say? There's nothing to which we can compare existing because none of us can remember ever *not* existing. It's hard to say anything very meaningful about it, yet, paradoxically, we could talk about it forever. Perhaps the most meaningful reply anyone could make would be, "Well, see for yourself!"

And that's what each of us has to do. Nobody can tell us what it is like to *be*. We know it through being.

I can know me only through being me.

I would like to invite you to examine the sensation directly. Examine your direct sense of being here now. "I am." What is the gut feeling of it?

Can you sense it? Does it feel tense and difficult? Does it feel easy as rain?

To find out, we have to inquire intuitively. We have to just sense it, without using words. "I am." It's right here, and I know it, but I find it hard to explain.

Can you sense that it goes far beyond language? It seems like a great mystery, and if we can celebrate that mystery if we can embrace it directly, we can open up like a budding flower.

It is so far beyond anything we can think or say that it defies description. All that we can say is, "I am." The direct sensation of being has no size, no shape, no color, and no attributes of any kind. It just is. All around this center of being are the many things that we can name and define, like our skin, our hair, our brain, our thoughts, our feelings, and our life story. Around our center of being, we can describe many things. "I am so many years old. I have done this. I would like to do that. I was born here, and my parents were..." and so on. And on and on and on.

These things move outward from that center, like the whorls of a sunflower head, spiraling out into florets, and bright petals. At the center of it, all is something seed-like, something unformed. "I am."

Thoughts may come up in the mind but the sensation of being comes before any one of those thoughts. Feelings may arise in our hearts or sensations in our body—but around all of that, underneath all of that, and in the middle of all these things, is being. Even the word. "being," doesn't do it justice.

It's so utterly obvious, the mind stops in its tracks.

Anything we can say about this deeply personal sense that "I am" is a movement away from the center point. It is here in this focus of conscious awareness, in the middle of the wheel of experiences, in the eye of the great storm of our entire lives, where we can find our doorway to self-knowledge. It is silent, alive, and full of energy. It is the source point of all we think, all we encounter, all we say, all we do.

It is where an artist goes for inspiration. It is the space we access when we pray or meditate. It is where our most powerful hunches and intuitions come from. It is where we feel, "I just *know*." It is deeper than even our dreams and our dreamless sleep. It comes before language, before learning, before school, before habits, and before conditioning. It is here when we are born and it is here at the moment of death.

All our lives we are flowing out of this "place," encountering everything else and flowing back into the same "place." Except that it's not a place at all, for, wherever we go, there it goes too. Whatever happens to us, there it is, with us. No matter what we plan, what we achieve, no matter at which things we fail, there it always is, as us, watching, living, as our source.

Each of us experiences our self as the center point of existence. The whole universe, the whole world of people and things, appears to us in our center of perception.

Every living being experiences existence in this way. Each of us is like an aperture in the universe, looking at itself, the cosmos at large, from a unique vantage point.

The sense of self is mirror-like. It reflects that which is outside of itself and the world sends a reflection back again. This is why we are so interested in how other people perceive us. We want to know what we are, so we search for reflections out there. We know ourselves "in here" by looking at our reflection "out there." The strange thing is, we experience *everything* "in here."

We can have a sense of self that is open and accommodating or a sense of self that is closed and limited. It can feel complicated or it can feel as easy as breathing.

Right here in this cosmic doorway, in this mysterious, mirror aperture of awareness, is our link to love.

The love is already here, expressed *as us*. It is only that we have temporarily forgotten what we are. We have become lost in thoughts and beliefs about who we are and feelings about what we are not, but underneath all of those thoughts and feelings is a love of being. "I am."

When this sense of "I am" feels closed and constricted or fearful, we feel highly individualized. Separated at birth. We feel cut off from the "other." We feel lonely and unloved or threatened. We feel detached and vulnerable. We feel as if we are existing in a bubble and we need to protect our bubble of existence.

As a result, our bodies become tense, on a very deep level. We find ourselves behaving badly, eating badly, and living badly. Our thinking becomes self-critical and toxic. We become unbalanced and usually something goes wrong. Either we become sick or something in life gives us a knock. The self is mirror-like. It reflects our state of being from the world outside. When there is trouble inside, all we see outside is trouble.

When the sense of "I am" is relaxed, confident, expansive, and open, it embraces all things outside of itself in an open and friendly way. It is curious, deeply interested, and adventurous. This is when we feel that we have spontaneously arisen out of some kind of nurturing ocean of existence, like an individual wave. It feels strange, maybe, but it feels like fun, and it feels rewarding to exist, to explore what could be. We get that feeling of being connected to the whole universe and finding our unique riff in the harmony of the totality of things. It is an inner "Yes!" to our core self.

As a result, our bodies are deeply relaxed and they heal more quickly. We find ourselves behaving in uplifting, helpful ways, eating what nourishes us, and living well. There is no real trouble inside, so as a reflection, there is no real trouble "out there" either. We become balanced and, although there are still challenges in life, we meet those challenges with courage and heart. We begin to outwardly manifest joy and abundance from an inner space of joy and abundance.

This is really what it means to love oneself.

First, we get to know what we are, deep down in our roots. It's more like remembering than getting to know something for the first time. The fact is that we have always been what we are. All we have to do is look inside again.

We find a kind of a mystery there, but we can sense it intuitively and an inner door opens. We relax into that sense of being—just as we are—and the love begins to flow all by itself. We appreciate the mystery, the complexity, the wonder of just this—just being "me." We love to be—whatever we are—and so we begin to love the things, the beings, the events, the circumstances around us too.

Little children cannot yet know what they are. They have to absorb so many things and, as they are absorbing the whole world around them, they slowly begin to rediscover what they are inside. It's a process that develops naturally over the years.

At some point, we might lose our connection and lose our way. We misplace our inner compass. We are so focused on the life outside of us that we forget the life inside of us.

Come back home for a visit sometime. Loving yourself is the doorway to cosmic love, the greatest love affair of all time.

To love the self is to love all. To know the self is to know all. To accept the self, cherish the self, and be at peace within the self, is to come back into the universe, our true home. It makes us feel real. It makes us able to engage with reality, in a friendly and open way, as if we are on a permanent holiday.

When we experience something awesome, the first thing we want to do is to share it with someone. That is the beauty of this paradox of self-love. It transcends the "small, limited" self. It is not the same as narcissism because it is genuine. It doesn't come from a deep sense of lack, a sense of "maybe I'm not good enough." Instead, it comes from an abundance of natural love energy. It emerges from the recognition of harmony and unity. The first thing we want to do when we remember our true selves is to share.

Self-love is self-unity because love is unity. An integrated, unified self feels love. A loving self feels unified.

This is what people sense and what they know when they go through a mystical experience or a spiritual awakening. This is the message from all the greatest spiritual teachers. This is the truth that modern psychology is just beginning to unravel. This is what people have held in their hearts since the beginning of recorded history. To know the self deeply and intimately, to love the self fully, is to know this too.

The source of you is nothing other than love. Your final destination is nowhere else than love. You are safe. You are beloved. You are worthy. You are deserving. You are a celebration of individuality, joined forever to all things as one. You are so much more than you could ever imagine. Your story is cosmic in scope and breadth. There is nothing to fear, nowhere to go to feel complete, except right here, in your center point of being.

The universe delights in you as much as you delight in the universe, for you are joined at the source. The love you seek from other people is only a reflection of this same true love. The things that fill your heart with a glow, the things that switch you on, the things that lift you—are all reflections of this mirror-like love.

Just fall back into it, and know. Take a deep breath, smile, and tell yourself: "I love you".

You are a radiant embodiment of love, intricately woven into the fabric of the universe.

Your journey begins and ends within the embrace of love, your true home.

Within the depths of your being, you are safe, cherished,

and deserving of all the love and joy that life has to offer.

Your individuality is a brilliant celebration, forever connected to the fabric of existence.

Expand your vision, for you are so much more than you can fathom.

Your story echoes through the cosmos, resonating with the beauty of creation.

Release all fear, for in your center point of being, you are complete.

Embrace this truth, fall effortlessly into the arms of love,

and bask in the boundless bliss that awaits.

CHAPTER 16

THE INNER SANCTUARY: EMBRACING SELF-LOVE

Self-love requires no effort, no plan, no luck.

It's more like falling backward

into the arms of someone you trust,

Someone you love.

Someone you know will catch you -

Your very own self.

To get to this point of release, we have to surrender our small, egoic, fearful ideas of "me" and fall back into that feeling of natural acceptance, gratitude, and appreciation for what we already are. It requires us to carry the joyful, accepting spirit of our inner child in the arms of a wise, resilient, and caring adult.

It is the ultimate leap of faith. It is an act of such intimate trust. It takes a great tenderness of heart.

To realize Nirvana is to realize that *this is it*. It's all right here. This is heaven, this is paradise—if only we have the eyes to see it.

Don't let your failures or your heartaches define your life. We need to drink in the moments we are living now or we will monotonously go through our life never really feeling like we "made it" or that we are finally happy.

We knew it in our bones when we were children, but somehow the world made us forget and we lost the wonder in our eyes. We started looking at distractions, we started believing in fears. We tended a garden of inadequacies inside us and built a fence of musts and must-nots.

Remember who you are. Find your barefoot, child-like brilliance. It's still there. Remember your core self. Trust it.

Your core, essential self arrived on this world scene all by itself. You didn't have to force it to happen. You didn't make a mistake. The events that led to "you" are so far beyond your control, so cosmic in scale, that it makes no sense to speak about blame. Arising along with the inevitability that happens to be shaped like "you," there is also a sense that you are co-creating your life.

We are participants in the creation process, whether we are willing or unwilling participants, whether we create unconsciously, or consciously.

We are co-creating our problems. We are co-creating our joys. Become aware of, become deeply interested in what you are creating as you.

Yes, your parents indeed played a part in providing your chassis, your physical framework. Yes, it is true that, when you were a small child, you were dependent on them to feed you, nourish you, and teach you. It is true that you are a part of this world and you depend on others to meet needs that you cannot meet yourself. It is certainly true that you cannot control everything that happens in this world. It is true that the world is full of pitfalls, dangers, threats, and complications.

Even so, here you are.

Something breathed your very first breath. It was not your ego, it was not your *idea* of something you were supposed to become, something defective, or something planned in your infant brain. It just happened. Something caused you to grow up. Something is beating your heart. Something is blinking your eyes, moving your fingers, walking your steps.

Weirdly enough, the moment that we become conscious that we are doing something, we feel as if we are doing it. When it is unconscious, it feels as if it is doing us, or just happening to us.

Sometimes we feel that we are in control, other times we feel helpless.

We can hold our sense of control in life the way a construction worker holds a sledgehammer, the way a police officer holds a gun or the way an artist holds a fine brush.

A very big part of what happens in us, through us, and by means of us is happening spontaneously, effortlessly, and without the need of ego control. We trust it to happen, although we become very alarmed when something goes wrong. The rest of the time, it is taken for granted. Life is doing its thing, there in the background.

Yet here you are.

You're alive, swimming in the stream of your whole lifetime, however long that may last.

Remember your source. Remember your destination because it is *you*.

Remember what life really is and fall back into love with life.

Resistance to the stream of life is simply a state of mind. It is a condition of forgetfulness. Allow me to illustrate the meaning here.

Has it happened to you that a song suddenly comes to life? It often happens during the "honeymoon stage" of a love affair. A song will start playing and, even though we know the song, we know all the lyrics, even though we have heard that same song on the radio a hundred times, suddenly it seems as if we are hearing the song for the first time.

"I never realized how beautiful this song is!" we think to ourselves. It is an unexpected thing, like walking into the garden to discover a flower that was not there the day before.

We know some of the words, but now suddenly those words, and that familiar melody, touch our hearts in a new kind of way. The song was always there, in our memory, and we could have analyzed it if we wanted to, but this is different. The song now seems to have a deep beauty and truth in it. Now it feels as if the song is all about our very own experience of love. It feels like it was written for us, by us, somehow. It gives wings to our hearts.

In reality, it's the same tune, but now something inside of us has changed. We have opened in some way. Somehow, we have grown, or become more attentive. We have "fallen in love." We have become more receptive to a subtle energy field. We can appreciate the nuances, and the grace of the song because we are listening with new ears.

A similar thing happens after a breakup. We hear one of those sad breakup songs and we know the song well, but suddenly it is as if we hear the words for the first time and we think, "I know your pain. I know it deeply: I wonder if anybody else can hear how powerful the lyrics of this song are!" The song can express everything you feel in your heart, but cannot.

It's a new feeling of connection, on a heart level, and it transcends the rational. It has a living quality.

Falling back into love with life happens in this same kind of underground and unexpected way. It's the old familiar tune of life, but now we feel its depth, its poignancy, tenderness, its power, its vibrancy. Now it makes sense, in a brand-new way.

We are still in the same body. We still have the same brain, containing the same memories. We still face the same world, with the same circumstances; the same bills need to be paid, and the same options are available for dinner, but now something inside of us has changed. All begins to shine.

The heart has an incredible transformative power. It is close to magic. We can open up, and see life for the wonder that it is once again, no matter how many years ago we forgot. A room can be dark for a century, but light a candle, and the darkness is instantly gone.

Fall back into yourself. You're right here, waiting to catch you.

Trust the rhythm of your life the way you trust your heart to beat, the way you trust the breath coming in and going out. Trust your ability to live well, the way you trust nature to fall asleep in winter and wake up in spring.

Trust that you are going to cope, that you are going to thrive, despite the challenges, and the way the nails on your fingers keep on growing, no matter how many times you cut them. Trust yourself, trust that you will be there for you, the way you trust that the stars will be there in the sky above, even if you can't see them right now.

You have never gone anywhere. You have never failed to be you. Here you are, being you. Trust that.

Allow the self-judgments to fall away just as autumn leaves fall. Allow the self-criticisms to melt, just as the snow melts on a warm day.

Allow the dreams of the future to unfold on their own timetables, in their own ways, the way you trust sleep to come at night and wakefulness to come in the morning.

Fall back in love with your very own life-stream. See the rippling wonder that you are, without adding a drop. See how nourishment flows within you, from you, and through you. See how you are interacting with this vast cosmos, here on solid ground, in your own unique way, just as you are. Follow the landscape down to the ocean, trusting that you are heading in the right direction. Fall with it. Flow with it. Swim in it like a child.

Stop fighting so hard to be perfect and simply fall back in love with your relationships. See the love in your children's eyes and allow that light to ignite a sense of wonder in you again. See the patience and compassion in your relationship with your spouse and allow that to fill your heart again. Trust your gut. Trust your heart. Trust your life.

Fall in love with your job, or quit and start doing what you have always wanted to do. You can't break, you can't disappear overnight, you won't shatter, and you will not dissolve into mist.

Fall right back in love with your problems, all your glitches and your quirks; fall into a state of love, in and around all the things you criticize about yourself, all the things you hate about you, all the problems you imagine are yours, and all the things that you dislike about your life, and see what happens.

If you fall into a state of conscious love with your anger, then the anger transforms into raw energy. It becomes something new, something available to use in a new way, and it can supercharge your growth, or your actions to remedy a situation. The frustration becomes construction. The destructive becomes creative—through love.

Surround your inadequacy with that same feeling of acceptance and love, and see what happens. Instead of a harsh judgment, it changes. It's now as if we're talking to a beloved child who feels inadequate and we become encouraging, supportive, and inspiring to ourselves, instead of self-critical. That one small difference—the love feeling, the acceptance, the non-judgment—makes all the difference.

Fall in love with your appearance, no matter how old, disheveled, or unworthy you feel. See how a new inner glow appears. Fall in love with your state of health, your financial status, your position in life, your level of education, and any other thing in life that feels incomplete, wrong, or unsatisfactory. The most amazing thing happens: I changes. The outer circumstances remain as they are, but something new appears, an original, uncaused kind of energy. The lyrics of the same song now hold a new meaning.

Jealousy is easily transmuted into admiration in this same way. Mean, nasty competition becomes a beautiful collaboration. Decay becomes renewal. Animosity becomes friendly sparring, leading to a deeper bond with a shared focus. Self-loathing becomes self-acceptance, and it changes into inspiration, instead of fear or regret.

Fall back into love with your fear and it somehow becomes your courage.

Fall back into love with your sadness and it somehow becomes your wisdom.

Fall back into love with your loss and it somehow becomes your treasure.

Fall back into love with your very own life; it becomes a celebration of you and everyone else is invited to the celebration too.

Fall back into love with *where* you are, *what* you are, *when* you are, and *how* you are. Look around you and try to see how gorgeous it all is, how *weird* it all is, how full of possibilities if only we don't judge things.

And, for heaven's sake, don't lose that love in an idea, in a dream, or in another person.

CHAPTER 17

RECLAIMING THE SOURCE WITHIN

We can lose our connection. We can lose touch with that feeling of simple, natural well-being and wholeness. We can lose the direct experience of our own love. Why does it happen to us?

It happens because we mistake the source of love for a reflection and we go deaf to the echoes of understanding in our hearts. Do any of the following scenarios sound familiar?

We invest our sense of completion in outward things that may or may not happen. "If I win, there will be justice and I will be complete. Then I will be happy."

We identify our sense of purpose and belonging with others. "He was my whole world, he was my reason, but now he has gone. Now I don't find joy in anything anymore."

We invest our permission to be happy in events outside of our control. "I was so happy for just a moment, I thought it had finally happened—but then it all disappeared and now I am even more miserable than before."

We pin our internal happiness on an outcome, a final destination. "We tried for so long. Finally, we just had to accept that it is never going to happen. You know, I don't know how I can go on, but I just have to."

We mistake the complexities, the constant stream of activities, the never-ending bombardment of responsibilities and duties on the circumference of our lives—we mistake them for our center. "My life has degenerated into a nightmare of chores. I feel like a robot, and I'm living my life on autopilot. All I do is take care of the kids and do what needs to be done—there's no time left for ME."

We lose ourselves in the love of another. "I gave him my whole heart and soul and I gave my children everything, and now it seems as if I lost myself along the way."

We tie our happiness up in the expected responses from other people. "I don't deserve to be treated this way! All I ever do is help, nurture, and give—and this is the way you treat me!"

We misunderstand something important. We believe that our source of love depends on the acknowledgment of other people. "Nobody sees me. Nobody seems to know that I exist anymore.

I get no respect, I don't get treated the way I treat other people. It's not fair."

We sell our joy to an idea, and the idea can evaporate at any moment. We forget that, underneath that idea, life itself is real. That which experiences the living is the real thing, and it is dependable and unchanging. Events come and go. Relationships change. Circumstances change. Thoughts and dreams come and go, and we—the real, living, loving, laughing beings—we remain through it all.

Deep down there is a fear and it holds us back, closing up our love channels. It is the fear of not being enough, not being in the right place, the fear that somehow we made a life mistake somewhere. We fear that we are not going to live the way we always wanted to. We're not going to get to experience the things we so badly wanted. We fear that we are not loved as we need to be loved, just for who we are. We fear that we do not deserve to exist—but it's a misunderstanding.

Don't let that fear, that misunderstanding cloud your insight.

You are that love. It is you. It's what you are made of.

It is the mysterious, vital glow within your human pattern of being, clothed with matter, surrounded by circumstances in this world, swimming through the stream of your very own lifetime.

You are a miracle of existence, in the shape of you and what you give to the world, just by being here, just by being the real you—is beyond measure. We all need you, just as you need all of us.

Your real happiness, your core, essential love, does not depend on another person. It does not depend on any outward circumstance. It does not need a specific outcome. To have power, to feel real and sustaining, it does not have to be acknowledged by anyone in this world—except you.

When we acknowledge our true essence, we see that it is shaped like love. It is open, accepting, nurturing, wholesome, and full of vibrant, living energy. When we recall it here inside of us, we remember that we have great power. We begin to radiate this energy, sun-like, without reservation. It becomes a blessing to all those we encounter. It seeps into the fabric of our lives, into the tiny details, the smallest gestures, the most seemingly inconsequential things. It becomes a glowing background to our entire lives.

Allow the naturally arising beauty of your life to outshine the darkness of your life circumstances.

Your physical body is a marvelously intricate vehicle for your experience. It is based on an ancient template, the template of life on this gorgeous, rich, and interesting planet. It goes beyond even that and expresses something unique about you as well. Your body has a natural intelligence. It does not fear those ideas. It is not stuck on outcomes. It does not worry about acknowledgment from others.

It flows and heals, and it knows.

Be like that. Just as you are.

Your emotions are power. They are currents of energy that thrill through your nervous system, through your heart, and your sense of feeling. Allow those emotions to unfold like flowers, without injuring them, without forcing them, without neglecting them, without labeling them with negative definitions. See how those emotions energize your journey. See how that flow of energy fills your senses.

Your thoughts are little points of light in the dark. See their cosmic beauty as they arrange themselves in constellations within your brain, available to your incredible power of awareness. Do not let those thoughts compel you in any way, they are not enemies, they are not final judgments of who you are. Tomorrow new thoughts will arrive. Let them be, let them shine, learn their interesting languages, and dance with their strange melodies. Let them go.

You are beyond all of these. You exist in the middle of the body, the emotions, the thoughts, and right at the center point of all your experiences of life.

You are the center point of love in your own life.

Coming from this grace, the truth once again remembers itself. All those things that seemed so wrong, so unfair, so painful, so disastrous, now find a place within this grace. Your soul brothers and sisters have always been your pillars of support, even though you forgot. Those who love you unconditionally were always there, even though you didn't see it. They were there in your corner, rooting for you. Their presence in your life is like sunshine.

In your journey, true friend soulmates weave threads of unwavering love, acceptance, and understanding. They are the ones who see beyond your flaws and celebrate your uniqueness. With them, you can bare your soul, knowing that they will hold your vulnerabilities with tenderness and compassion. They are the ones who stand by your side, not just in moments of triumph, but also in moments of doubt and struggle.

These soulmates are your guardians of the heart, the ones who remind you of your inherent worthiness, even when you forget. They reflect your brilliance back to you, illuminating the path of self-love and self-acceptance. They listen without judgment, hold space for your growth, and offer a steady hand to lift you up when life's winds try to knock you down.

Lean on these true friends, for they are your refuge in times of uncertainty and your champions of resilience. They hold the mirror to your beauty, reminding you of the strength and resilience that resides within. Their love is a beacon of light, guiding you home to the depths of your own heart.

Welcome the connections that go beyond superficialities, for these soulmate friendships are sacred gifts. Nurture these bonds with care, for they have the power to nurture your soul in return. Together, you create a symphony of support, encouragement, and growth, igniting each other's spirits to reach new heights.

Remember that you are not alone on this journey. You are surrounded by a tribe of soulmates, linked by the invisible threads of love and destiny. Open your heart to receive the love that flows freely from these cherished connections. Allow their presence to uplift you, inspire you, and remind you of your own greatness.

In the embrace of your true friend soulmates, you find solace, belonging, and a sense of home. Cherish these bonds, for they are the living embodiment of love's infinite power. Together, you create a symphony of authenticity and acceptance, forging a path toward self-love that radiates outward, touching the lives of all you encounter.

So, my dear friend, celebrate and honor these soulmates who journey alongside you. Lean on their unwavering support. Reciprocate their love with your whole heart. Together, you will continue to navigate the vast expanse of self-discovery, cultivating a profound connection that transcends time and space. You are blessed with true friend soulmates who illuminate your path with love, and in their presence, you discover the immense power of connection, acceptance, and the enduring bond of friendship.

There is so much love and light in this world if only we choose to see it again. Follow that light, for it leads to only one destination—your real, eternal home.

When we acknowledge our true essence, we see that it is shaped like love. It is open, accepting, nurturing, wholesome, and full of vibrant, living energy. When we recall it here inside of us, we remember that we have great power. We begin to radiate this energy, sun-like, without reservation. It becomes a blessing to all those we encounter. It seeps into the fabric of our lives, into the tiny details, the smallest gestures, the most seemingly inconsequential things. It becomes a glowing background to our entire lives. Allow the naturally arising beauty of your life to outshine the darkness of your life circumstances.

CHAPTER 18

LOVE AS THE GUIDING COMPASS: FOLLOWING THE WAY HOME

Following my love for all of my life.

It was only one love that showed me the way,

She sang, she danced, she waited, she called,

Drawing me ever inward,

Guiding me all the way home.

All your life you have been following your love. Maybe you did not know it. Maybe you suspected that it was so but doubted your intuition. Maybe you forgot. All the while, love was there, prompting you, urging you, calling to you, inviting you, beckoning, whispering, nudging, and playfully hiding away so that you could enjoy finding her.

You followed her toward the first friendships you forged. You followed her in the games you used to love to play, into the adventures you went on as a child. You discovered her in the garden, in the sunshine, splashing in the water, walking in nature, and laughing your head off at unexpected and weird things that happened. You heard her voice in the stories that stuck with you, those stories that filled you with awe, wonder, curiosity, and inspiration. She lit the lights behind your eyes. She made you want to explore, and taste life.

You followed her toward the things you chose over the things you did not choose.

You followed love toward important things, like a genuine urge for spiritual guidance, but she guided you in all kinds of normal, everyday ways too. You followed your love toward your music choices, outfit choices, subject choices while studying, your career choices, and it led you straight into your love affairs. It led you right into trouble and right through the middle of it and out the other end, unscratched, toward wisdom, and through all the pages of a wonderful story—the story of your whole life.

Love is a compass needle. It shows the way. It leads you where you're supposed to go and it has led you to where you are now. Trust it, and follow it to the end.

One end of the compass needle points to the things in life that just feel right. It feels something like acceptance, adventure, inspiration, gratitude, well-being, wholeness, sharing, growing, laughing, and enduring. It's not always a perfect, rational pinpoint destination, but the general direction is clear.

The other end of the compass needle points the other way. It feels more like judgment, dullness, stickiness, dissatisfaction, and unease, incompleteness, hoarding, decaying, fearing, and giving up. It doesn't always point at a specific pathway but it lets you know, in no uncertain terms, that you are going in the wrong general direction.

We can't always explain in our minds why we feel these guiding feelings, but they are real. They appear to us in our dreams, in our waking emotions, in our intuition, and in our bodies too. We might sense it in the pit of the stomach, in the heart area, or the whole body. It feels uncomfortable, prickly, or magnetic, and we just want to follow, the way a bee is drawn to a flower.

We are taught and conditioned to think rationally, to plan before we leap, and to weigh the pros and cons before we make an important decision. There is merit and wisdom in that, no doubt.

But think of this: How often has it been your experience that you think things through obsessively for a long time until you are totally confused by all the pros and cons, and you have thought about so many possible outcomes, so many "what if's" that you are completely lost, and then just make a snap judgment. The rational, planning mind cannot see every possible outcome.

Following your love doesn't mean that you make senseless decisions without weighing things internally. It means that you learn to trust your intuition after weighing all the facts. The heart compass is a friend of the wisdom of life experience. It knows all about mistakes. It is ancient and wise, not naïve.

When that feeling of inspiration arises, where does it come from? Do we need to explain it?

We feel the urge to do something. Maybe we want to paint, craft, run, write something, or learn something. Maybe we want to explore a part of the world or learn how to play a musical instrument. Whatever the inspiration, it feels exciting and wholesome, and it energizes our whole being.

Follow it. Follow it to the end because our compass needle is pointing out the best direction for you at this moment.

It may eventually lead to a dead end or a mistake. So be it. In that dead end, in that mistake, will be another opportunity and the road that led there was the whole reason. Along the way, we will gain an experience that is beyond value and we will miss it if we decline.

We have these urges and feelings for a reason. They are our angels, our ascended gurus, our mentors, our animal spirit guides, and our ancestors. It doesn't matter one bit what we call them, but they are speaking to us through the cracks of this world, whispering to our hearts, offering timeless understanding.

Listen to that echo. It is a message coming from a reflection of you, another piece of you, from a deeper place. Learn how to listen, and learn to trust it fully.

To trust this feeling is to trust the highest, purest sense of self, and to be unified on the inside. To doubt it is to cause self-division and to live from indecision, timidity, resistance, and regret.

Only you know what you would love to do. Only you can judge what that means and why it is important. Only you can get there in your own way and only you can know what it is like to say no or to say yes to this moment, for you.

Those of us who are full of energy are here to help you, just as you will help us again when your energy is full and overflowing. Love builds these wonderful bridges of reciprocation because it delights in sharing.

That feeling of compassion that rises inside us is a clue. It is our compass needle, showing us where our love wants to go. When we ignore it, we start feeling a sense of guilt and a kind of hopelessness, full of internal justifications: "What use is what I say or do? I'm small and the world is so big, with so many troubles. What can I do? It's pointless."

That's when we start forgetting about our compass.

When that feeling of being stuck, that we're somehow going in the wrong direction, comes up, that's our clue. Our compass is working. We can ignore it and justify our choice in a hundred ways, but the feeling doesn't go away.

Listen to the echoes of knowing in your heart. Trust your compass.

It's not there to fix your life. It is there to give you feedback on your choices, and to guide you through the changing landscape of decisions and actions. It's not there to judge you as good or bad. It's there to resonate, to echo, to be a sounding board for your energy, your vibe, and your engagement. Above all, it wants to help. It is a friendly and useful tool and a great ally. You are always free to listen or ignore it—it will go on sending those messages, resonating, echoing your truth for you and nobody else. It shows you your very own center of balance.

Authentic, unconditional love sees no right or wrong choices. It sees no completely good or completely evil people. It embraces all things and works within whatever happens to be at hand in the most positive, uplifting way it can. It can adapt anywhere and at any time. Like water, it can find its way into the tiniest cracks and seep in everywhere. It always moves, always nourishes, and always has a cleansing and edifying nature. It never condemns your mistakes. It never labels you. It sets you free.

It sets you free to explore, to make choices, and to embark on the incredible journey of your life. Love, with its unwavering presence and gentle guidance, is the key to unlocking your true potential. It calls upon you to live a life that aligns with your deepest desires and resonates with the essence of who you are.

When you listen to your heart's compass, you begin to notice the miracles that unfold before you. The synchronicities and serendipities that seem like mere coincidences become signs that you are on the right path. Love opens doors that you never thought existed, and it leads you to places you never thought you could reach.

Following your love requires courage, for it may lead you to unfamiliar territories and challenge you to step outside your comfort zone. Nevertheless, it is in those moments of uncertainty and vulnerability that you discover the depths of your strength and resilience. Love empowers you to embrace change and embrace the unknown with open arms, knowing that the journey itself holds countless treasures.

As you continue to follow your love, you become a beacon of inspiration for others. Your authenticity and unwavering commitment to living a life that resonates with your soul's calling become a guiding light for those who are still searching. You inspire them to listen to their hearts, to trust their intuition, and to embark on their unique paths of love and purpose.

Remember that the compass of love is not a one-time guide but a lifelong companion. It evolves as you grow and change, always pointing you in the direction that aligns with your highest good. Sometimes the path may seem difficult, and you may encounter obstacles and setbacks along the way. But love never abandons you. It continues to beckon you forward, encouraging you to rise above challenges and embrace the lessons they hold.

Through all the twists and turns, the triumphs and tribulations, love remains your steadfast guide. It whispers words of encouragement in moments of doubt, celebrates your victories, and holds you gently when you stumble. It reminds you that you are worthy of love and that by following your heart's compass, you are co-creating a life filled with purpose, joy, and fulfillment.

So, my dear friend, trust in the power of love. Embrace its guidance, for it is a gift that has been with you all along. Open your heart to the infinite possibilities that await, and allow love to weave its magic into the very fabric of your existence. Follow your love, and let it lead you to a truly extraordinary life.

21 ECHOES OF UNDERSTANDING: *GOLDEN PRINCIPLES FOR SELF-LOVE AND ACCEPTANCE*

1. You are a story that delights, inspires, and teaches the universe. Within you lies a captivating story that holds the power to captivate, inspire, and teach the universe. It is a tale of triumph over unique challenges, offering the world a glimpse into an extraordinary perspective. As the protagonist of your story, you hold the pen and have the privilege to shape the defining moments. How will you show up? How will you nurture the growth of your character?

2. You are rare and perfect. Embrace the beauty of your uniqueness, for there is nothing wrong with you. While we are all interconnected as one, the brilliance of creation lies in our diverse expressions. Release the judgments that bind you and allow your heart to express love in its authentic way, adding your unique brushstroke to the painting we call life.

3. Know what your ego is. Dive deep into the understanding of your ego, recognizing that it is not your true essence. You possess the power to redefine and reshape your ego, shedding its limitations and allowing it to operate in harmony with your higher self. Observe its workings and prevent it from ruling your being through fear, instead letting love take its rightful place on the throne of self.

4. Your worth cannot be quantified, compared, measured, limited, or nullified. Your worth defies quantification, comparison, and limitation. It emanates from your very essence, from your authenticity and presence in this world. Feel the warmth of worthiness in your heart, for it is not a measure to be weighed, but a truth to be embraced.

5. Nothing can define you, limit you, box you in, or force you into a rut. Refuse to be defined, confined, or boxed in by external forces. Your essence transcends the boundaries that society imposes. Embrace the limitless nature of your being and embrace each moment as an opportunity for growth and expansion. Do not allow any external definition to dictate your journey, for the power to define yourself resides solely within.

6. You cannot break. Understand that you are unbreakable. While the external aspects of life may change and transform, your core self remains untouched by any circumstance. Revel in the game of shedding the old and embracing the new, for your true self finds delight in the ever-evolving dance of existence.

7. You are constantly reinventing yourself by default. Embrace the inherent nature of constant reinvention. Notice the shifts and transformations that unfold within you, celebrate them, and flow with the rhythm of change. You are not stuck, for life courses through your veins, ensuring that you are always alive and open to new possibilities.

8. Make peace with the totality of yourself. Seek peace within the entirety of your being, for it is not an external pursuit but an internal sanctuary. Embrace all aspects of yourself—the light and the shadow—and find solace in the complete acceptance of who you are. It is within this acceptance that true peace resides.

9. Real motivation comes from the heart. True motivation arises from the depths of your heart. It nourishes, sustains, and carves a path through the challenges of life. Like water, it flows effortlessly toward the destinations that align with your purpose. Embrace the natural flow of inspiration and allow it to guide your actions.

10. You are your purpose. Realize that you are your own purpose. Your existence surpasses the realm of cause and effect.

Just as nature holds its intrinsic purpose, so do you. Embrace the magnificence of simply being and allow your authentic self to radiate its unique purpose into the world.

11. Self-love is self-knowledge, leading to self-unity. Self-love is an exploration of self-knowledge, leading to a profound sense of inner unity. Delve into the depths of your being, unraveling the layers of your existence. In this journey of self-discovery, you will find an infinite well of mystery. Within this knowing, you will uncover a profound sense of love and unity, embracing the wholeness that resides within.

12. Fall back into love with life. Fall back into love with life itself. Shift your inner state from yearning for what could be to cherishing what is right here, at this moment. Witness the alchemy that occurs within when you appreciate the present. It transforms your circumstances, illuminating the world around you with the golden glow of gratitude.

13. Follow your love. Allow your intuitive center, nestled within the depths of your heart, to be a trustworthy compass. Learn to attune to its whispers of inspiration. When you feel its gentle nudges, follow them with unwavering faith. Embrace the flow that comes from acting upon these intuitive insights and immerse yourself in the boundless possibilities that unfold.

14. Reconnect with your inner child. Remember the pure essence of who you were as a child. Reconnect with the innocent joy, the unadulterated sense of wonder, and the simple delight in being alive. Rediscover that childlike spirit within, for the answer to your true self is much closer than you think.

15. The self is mirror-like. Understand that you are a mirror, reflecting and being reflected by the world around you. The energy you project onto others is the energy that resonates within yourself. Approach life with love, compassion, and forgiveness, and witness how these qualities are mirrored back to you, creating a harmonious dance of interconnectedness.

16. You are not an idea. You are not an abstract idea confined to the thoughts of others. Release the limitations imposed by external perceptions and break free from the confines of self-imposed beliefs. Embrace the truth that lies beyond ideas and connect with the essence of your being.

17. Love has power and wisdom. Love holds immeasurable power and profound wisdom. When your heart is open to love, when you embrace the giving and receiving of love, the world begins to align and make sense. Love becomes the guiding force, allowing everything to harmoniously fall into place.

18. You create your unhappiness. You create your joy. Recognize that you hold the key to your happiness. You have the power to create joy or unhappiness within your being. Release the blame that serves as self-deception, and embrace the transformative power of taking responsibility for your emotions and experiences.

19. What other people think of you doesn't matter. The opinions of others hold little significance in defining your true worth. When others project their pain, fear, and division upon you, understand that it does not touch the core of your essence. Embrace your inherent worthiness, knowing that it is untainted by external judgment.

20. Imperfection is perfect. Imperfection is a testament to the perfection of your journey. Embrace the process of trying, failing, and trying again, for it is in these moments that growth and learning truly flourish. Failure is not a flaw, but an opportunity to embrace your perfectly imperfect nature.

21. You are deeply loved. Remember, deep within, that you are profoundly loved. You are safe, natural, and worthy of all the beauty life has to offer. Allow yourself to follow the compass of love, for it will guide you back to the place you truly belong—home within yourself.

And above all, remember that in the vast expanse of existence, your presence is a gift to the world. Your individual experiences, perspectives, and triumphs add vibrant hues to the collective canvas of humanity. Cherish the magnificence of your own story, for it holds the power to touch hearts, ignite souls, and inspire transformation.

As you navigate the ups and downs of life, hold steadfast to the truth that self-love is a continuous journey. It requires patience, compassion, and a willingness to embrace both the light and the shadow within. Through each step, each stumble, and each moment of growth, remember to extend grace to yourself. Embrace the lessons learned from both success and perceived failure, for they shape you into the resilient and extraordinary being that you are.

Embrace the power of self-love as a catalyst for change in the world. When you love and accept yourself fully, you radiate a contagious energy that uplifts and empowers those around you. By embodying your authentic truth, you permit others to do the same. In this ripple effect of self-love, we collectively weave a blanket of compassion, unity, and acceptance that wraps around all of us.

So, dear soul, embark on this journey of self-love with an open heart and an unwavering belief in your inherent worth. Embrace the profound truth that you are deserving of love, understanding, and self-compassion. Embrace the power of self-love, for it is the key that unlocks the extraordinary potential within you and paves the way for a life filled with purpose, joy, and boundless love.

CONCLUSION

This is my love letter to my soul sisters, my soul brothers, and my whole extended soul family. It is for every living being, for we are all connected on an energetic level. I hope that some of these words echo in your depths, awakening hope and insight. May they uplift your day in some small way.

These messages are for anyone who finds themselves in difficult life situations. It is for those who just feel lost in their life right now, cheated by fate, who feel as if they are missing out on life or overwhelmed by motherhood, young adulthood, endless repetitive patterns, chores, responsibilities, unfair life events, or those who feel stuck in their life. It is for those who have lost dear loved ones and feel as if life has lost its shine. It is here for my children and future generations as a little beacon of hope, a light in the night. May it be a fairy light on your night walk.

I just want you to remember, and to know in your bones, to recognize once again that life IS good.

I admit, it is difficult most of the time and we forget so often. I know that I forget and it helps me to remember these things, for they echo something true and real.

We forget how amazing it is to just be. We feel lost sometimes as if we have accidentally strayed off our path, but we are on our path and we choose it, again and again, each moment. Yes, it is true and I acknowledge this—sometimes it is painful and unfair, and even so, and maybe even because of that, there is so much magic in this world. People with big hearts overcome incredible challenges all the time. You can too. I believe in you because I believe in me and I sense that we share the same essence, somehow. I hope that this echo resonates with you too.

Amidst the magnificent mosaic of existence, we often seek external knowledge, exploring the world around us and acquiring information about all kinds of people and things. Yet, along this quest for knowledge, we must remember that real wisdom remains incomplete until we truly know ourselves—the knower.

Self-knowledge becomes the key that unlocks the doors to wisdom, hope, peace, and purpose. It is a journey of introspection, an inner exploration that reveals the depths of our being.

Within you lies a wellspring of wisdom that surpasses theories and words. It is a silent voice, a guiding light that emanates from the very core of your existence. Tap into this inner well of wisdom, for it is always there, ready to illuminate your path and provide the answers you seek. Trust in its presence, even in moments when it feels distant or dormant, for it is a steadfast companion on your journey.

There will be hard days that test your resilience and make you question your purpose. In those moments, remember that even amidst the challenges, there are moments of pure bliss awaiting you. Those "AHA" moments will arise, as if the universe itself is whispering in your ear, revealing the interconnectedness of your experiences.

With a smile on your face, you will understand that every twist and turn, every triumph and setback, has led you precisely to where you are meant to be.

Trust in yourself, dear friend, in the depths of your most primal self, even if it feels as if that essence is slumbering within you. It is here, right now, walking beside you, breathing with you, hoping, failing, and trying again.

Embrace the journey of self-discovery, for it is a sacred pilgrimage that brings you closer to the truth of who you are. As you navigate the ebbs and flows of life, remember that you are never alone. The essence of your being intertwines with the fabric of the universe and in that cosmic dance, you are guided, supported, and loved beyond measure.

So, embrace your individuality, embrace your journey, and embrace the magnificent being that you are.

Trust in the wisdom that resides within you and let it guide your steps. You are here for a purpose and every experience, both challenging and blissful, serves to shape and awaken the brilliance that lies within. Embrace your unfolding story, for you are the author and the protagonist, creating a narrative of self-love, growth, and boundless possibility.

Life is a fleeting and wondrous gift, a delicate symphony woven with threads of joy, sorrow, love, and growth. Each moment, each breath holds within it the potential for magic. The world around us is filled with breathtaking beauty, from the gentle rustle of leaves in the wind to the kaleidoscope of colors that paint the sky at sunset. Yet, time slips through our fingers like grains of sand and if we do not truly pause to embrace the magnificence of it all, we may find ourselves looking back with regret.

Let us seize the opportunity to immerse ourselves in the enchantment of existence. Open your heart to the miracles that surround you, for they are both abundant and fleeting. Savor the beauty of this moment, for before you know it, it will become a cherished memory.

May these words echo in your depths, inspiring hope, insight, and a renewed appreciation for the extraordinary beauty that lies within and all around you. May you embrace life fully and merely your existence, celebrating each breath as a precious gift. You are deserving, you are worthy, you are resilient, you are enough, you matter and you are beautiful my friend.

With heartfelt gratitude and love, may your journey be filled with joy, purpose, and boundless possibilities.

Let your light illuminate the world.

EPILOGUE

Dearly beloved self,

I am gathering myself together today to say goodbye to an old friend.

The self that I was yesterday served me so faithfully and I was a dear companion. I am going to miss me.

I had my moments, let me tell you. It wasn't all sunshine and roses. It took some time to get to know me, but once I did, there was nobody better to have on my side. I didn't always get along but I knew, deep down, I always had my back.

I had my faults, I am the first to admit, but above all, I was loyal and true to myself. I was always there for me, no matter how crazy my ideas, no matter how low, no matter how high—I stood with me, through it all. I inspired myself more times than I know. I am stronger than I think. I celebrate all that I have overcome for I have walked through fire without an extinguisher or water.

Dearly beloved, I shed no tears for me, because I carry my spirit with me today.

And as I say goodbye to that old me, I greet a new me with an open and kinder heart.

Welcome, beloved self of today, I trust you and admire you, and I know we will walk the road ahead together for a while, come what may, until the journey's end.

Thank you for joining me as I become whole.

May I let go in peace,

and trust the magic of new beginnings.

Made in the USA
Columbia, SC
16 September 2023